Leading a Successful Reading Program

Administrators and Reading Specialists Working Together to Make It Happen

Nancy DeVries Guth

Stephanie Stephens Pettengill

Stafford County Public Schools
Stafford, Virginia, USA

INTERNATIONAL
Reading Association
800 BARKSDALE ROAD, PO BOX 8139
NEWARK, DE 19714-8139, USA
www.reading.org

Director of Publications Dan Mangan
Editorial Director, Books and Special Projects Teresa Curto
Managing Editor, Books Shannon T. Fortner
Acquisitions and Developmental Editor Corinne M. Mooney
Associate Editor Charlene M. Nichols
Associate Editor Elizabeth C. Hunt
Production Editor Amy Messick
Books and Inventory Assistant Rebecca A. Zell
Permissions Editor Janet S. Parrack
Assistant Permissions Editor Tyanna L. Collins
Production Department Manager Iona Muscella
Supervisor, Electronic Publishing Anette Schütz
Senior Electronic Publishing Specialist R. Lynn Harrison
Electronic Publishing Specialist Lisa M. Kochel
Proofreader Stacey Lynn Sharp

Project Editor Charlene M. Nichols

Art Cover Design, Linda Steere; Cover Photographs, ©Digital Vision (top), ©PhotoDisc (bottom); Interior Photographs, Nancy DeVries Guth and Karyn Spahr; Interior Illustrations (Appendixes A and B), Stephanie Stephens Pettengill

Library of Congress Cataloging-in-Publication Data
Guth, Nancy DeVries.
  Leading a successful reading program : administrators and reading specialists working together to make it happen / Nancy DeVries Guth, Stephanie Stephens Pettengill.
      p. cm.
  Includes bibliographical references and index.
  ISBN 0-87207-579-6
  1. Reading--Remedial teaching. 2. Literacy programs. 3. School improvement programs. I. Pettengill, Stephanie Stephens, 1966- II. Title.
  LB1050.5.G865 2005
  372.43--dc22

                                                                    2005020166

To my supportive family—those with me who daily give encouragement, those members previously with me who gave me my love for literacy, and those yet to be with me who give me hope for a literate future—thank you all for your inspiration.

—Nancy DeVries Guth

To Bill and Janey Stephens for always believing in me and to Dave Pettengill for making me believe in myself.

—Stephanie Stephens Pettengill

Contents

Preface

A
S COAUTHORS OF THIS book, we have been challenged by our fellow educators to create an informative guide about establishing a literacy program for those responsible for the program at any school, at any level. In our roles as a literacy supervisor and a reading specialist, we often have been asked to provide a guide for administrators, reading specialists, and teachers, as each professional tries to establish a constructivist, responsive literacy program in these standards-based, challenging times. At first we were hesitant, suggesting that a literacy program for a school must be individual and molded to fit the needs and strengths of the school and community. However, after discovering the International Reading Association (IRA) position statement *Teaching All Children to Read: The Roles of the Reading Specialist* (2000), we realized that the model was extremely helpful in explaining the roles a reading specialist could and should be encouraged to assume in a school setting. We also realized that by sharing how we used and adapted this model, we could help other educators develop an effective schoolwide literacy program. For example, we adapted this model by adding an additional aspect—motivation—to the program model because without motivation to engage in reading and writing skills on a daily basis, literacy ability is meaningless. Motivation is critical to the success of our program. As time went on and we presented our model, we realized that sharing our experiences and literacy model could help others as they tried to develop a schoolwide literacy program.

The audience for this book includes reading specialists, aspiring reading specialists, and administrators and supervisors interested in designing or supporting a literacy program for their school. The school reading specialist is a key component of this program model. In all of our district literacy support programs—elementary, middle, and high school—the reading specialist serves as a highly skilled literacy coach to both teachers and to students—that is, the reading specialist works with teachers to plan instruction and works with students in flexible groupings within the regular classroom and occasionally in pull-out programs.

Consequently, we chose to write this guide in two voices: (1) the voice of the literacy supervisor, to explain why this model is effective, and (2) the voice of the reading specialist, to explain how this model is put into action. Determine your purpose as a reader and read accordingly. Do you want to see the program in action? If so, read the voice of the reading specialist first. Do you want to determine the role and responsibilities for a central office? If so, begin with the voice of the supervisor. Note that there may be instances when information repeats from chapter to chapter because some information is necessary as background for each topic, and recommended practices are recursive in nature.

This guide is not designed as a recipe book but as an example of a program model that works for us. This program model can provide a vision for the literacy supervisor as he or she tries to influence programs so no teacher and no student get left behind, without the benefit of positive, productive literacy instruction. These suggestions are based on our combined years of experience as classroom teachers, reading specialists, and a literacy supervisor; therefore, we suggest protocols, lessons, and ideas that have worked for us, but as we write, we are always evolving, changing, and modifying our plans based on the literacy needs and experiences of the staff and students at each individual school. However, some common requirements are a given, and those are clearly defined in each chapter. The examples of the creation of the program and the program in action throughout this book are based on experiences working in a middle school, but the ideas can be applied at the elementary or high school levels as well.

Chapter 1 sets the stage for using the school reading specialist in his or her many roles as a literacy leader and provides a brief overview of these roles. We believe that leadership, although one specific component of this model, touches each role within this model. Reading specialists are expected to work with teachers, administrators, and parents rather than just students in need of improvement as in the traditional pull-out model. Thus, the reading specialist can be seen as the building-level expert, an integral part of each grade level and every academic team. Chapters 2, 3, and 4 describe the different ways the reading specialist can function as a school-based literacy leader. Chapter 2 describes how to develop and coordinate a schoolwide literacy program. We discuss how to design a schoolwide literacy vision, establish a school literacy committee, and get all staff involved. Chapter 3 provides details about how to develop a comprehensive literacy community within the school and how to work with all staff members as valued and contributing members of the literacy team. Chapter 4 describes how to build the school resource collection, respond to staff needs by assisting teachers in matching materials to state curriculum guidelines, and work with staff preferences and student needs.

Chapters 5 and 6 focus on the next category of the model—diagnosis and assessment. Assessment is the foundation of every successful comprehensive literacy program, when multiple results are used appropriately in collaboration with all team players—teachers, guidance counselors, students, and parents. We specifically discuss schoolwide assessment in chapter 5. Chapter 6 describes ways to use this assessment information in collaborative planning with teachers and provide this information to students and parents. Sharing reading and writing strategies and books on each student's instructional level is imperative if each student is to progress in his or her literacy development.

Powerful instruction is well planned and requires careful organization; therefore, chapter 7 includes suggestions for successfully organizing instruction. We provide appropriate, data-driven instructional decisions—based on our experiences and state and national requirements. Chapter 8 focuses on the most familiar aspect of the reading specialist's job—that of providing specialized instruction for small groups of students. We discuss how students with varied abilities can go to the reading specialist and how this arrangement can become a natural part of a school's literacy program.

Chapter 9 discusses motivation, including our reading incentives and summer reading initiative. We suggest ideas for stimulating motivation for staff, students, and parents—for reading enjoyment as well as practice. We believe we saved the best for last, the fun and the fuel for our success with staff, students, and parents. Finally, we bring closure to our suggestions and summarize the strengths and potential power of a comprehensive literacy program with a reading specialist involved in all aspects of the program.

Appendix A details the active thinking strategy PIRATES. Appendix B follows with sample lessons designed and used successfully by the reading specialist. These classroom lessons include strategies for before, during, and after reading and for test taking in subject area exams as well as standardized tests.

Our resource model of the reading specialist is based on our years of experience and supported by best practices. Make it your own, and it will work for you.

CHAPTER 1

The Reading Specialist as a Literacy Leader

"[I]f we are ever going to achieve research-based practice, then more than anything we need rich and detailed accounts that link important research to classroom practice and that show what that practice looks like when teachers do it well."

Pearson, 2000, p. 7

"SHE [OR HE] WENT that way" is the greeting I usually receive from school receptionists when I walk into one of the 26 schools in my rapidly growing school district. The person to whom the receptionist is referring is the school-based reading specialist. Keeping track of this individual has become an occasional source of humor as well as frustration for the school receptionist, but as a supervisor, a source of constant satisfaction. I joke with the reading specialists at our monthly staff meetings that they are not paid to stay in one place; as a supervisor, I expect them to be in constant motion because they provide literacy support to all of the people in the school.

Most teachers welcome literacy support from a colleague as they strive to achieve the high literacy expectations required by local, state, and national mandates. Making adequate yearly progress, achieving minimum standards with all subgroups of the population, having highly qualified teachers, using only evidence-based materials—all of these legislative mandates have raised expectations for every public school in the past few years. These mandates directly affect classroom teachers because they influence the use of specific materials and create higher expectations from school boards and parents, as well as additional staff development requirements. Well-prepared teachers who are confident, competent, and enthusiastic about teaching reading are essential if these state and national educational goals are to be met, according to *Teaching All Children to Read: The Roles of the Reading Specialist*, a position statement from the International Reading Association (IRA; 2000). Another position statement from IRA, *Investment in Teacher Preparation in the United States* (2003), points out the variability in the preparation and competence in beginning teachers. This position statement states that teacher preparation in teaching reading can vary from as many as 24 hours of semester work in reading to as little as 3 hours. The position statement also states that for literacy coaches—a position recently implemented as a strategy to help these teachers—training requirements can vary from a master's degree in literacy education to one seminar in reading methods. Many teachers who have earned degrees prior to 21st-century research do not know the latest literacy strategies or how to assist students from various literacy backgrounds. A certified reading specialist can be a valuable training resource for both new and seasoned staff members. In our program model, the reading specialist serves as a mentor to teachers, serves as a literacy coach to teachers and students, and provides guidance for the entire literacy program of the school. The literacy program is all encompassing, including reading, writing, listening, speaking, and viewing in all content areas, as well as in English class. Thus, when we refer to the reading program, we are referring to part of the school's comprehensive literacy program.

Literacy Expectations for Students

While more demands are being placed on teachers, higher level performance demands are also being placed on students. Literacy performance demands for students are increasing daily. The definition of literacy is in itself evolving, now including visual literacy and computer literacy, as well as reading and writing. Literacy derives from the Latin *litteratus*, which, in Cicero's time, meant a learned person. In current usage, the term implies an interaction between social demands and individual competence. Thus, the levels of literacy required for social functioning can and has varied across cultures and even across time within the same culture. Functional literacy, the level of learning at which one is able to read well enough to complete everyday life demands and activities, consists of continually evolving requirements for all students, regardless of background or economics (Venezky, 1995). Teachers are being asked to achieve higher proficiency levels with all students because standards at all levels are challenging students and teachers to accomplish more (O'Neal & Kapinus, 2000).

As the requirements for reading competence continue to rise in the United States, so does the knowledge required to teach all aspects of reading. Teaching reading may resemble a combination of rocket science and creative arts. Just when teachers think they have a workable curricular plan, changes such as new curriculum requirements and additional students frustrate them. Helping teachers meet this challenge is a constant struggle for administrators who are mired in the demands of organizing and running a small company—a company often with more than 1,000 students with varied backgrounds and abilities. Someone needs to be available to help teachers meet this challenge, to work with the media specialist, to assist the building administrator, and to advise parents and special educators. In our school district, this skillful and personable individual is the school-based reading specialist.

Expectations for the Reading Specialist

In my experience—and as research indicates—the role of the reading specialist may be as widely interpreted as the definition of literacy (Bean,

2004; "Coaches, Controversy, Consensus," 2004). In our school district, the role is crafted around the demands of the particular school, but with some clear expectations. This book is organized around these expectations or four key roles of the reading specialist in the literacy program model—that of providing (1) leadership, (2) instruction, (3) assessment, and (4) reading motivation (see Figure 1.1). We describe how to maximize the effect of reading specialists as they serve students and teachers while maintaining consistency and using research-based practices (see Table 1.1 for a list of responsibilities for reading specialists).

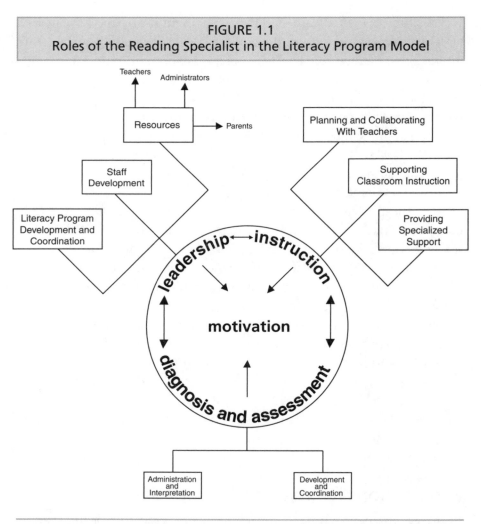

FIGURE 1.1
Roles of the Reading Specialist in the Literacy Program Model

Adapted from International Reading Association. (2000). *Teaching all children to read: The roles of the reading specialist.* A position statement of the International Reading Association. Newark, DE: Author.

TABLE 1.1
Responsibilities of the Reading Specialist

1. Share instructional suggestions.
The reading specialist should meet with all grade-level teams at least once every two weeks and assist with curriculum maps, pacing, and planning.

2. Collaborate for content area teaching.
The reading specialist should help teachers with lessons that focus on reading and writing in the content areas.

3. Provide on-site staff development.
The reading specialist should have the opportunity to collaborate on reading strategy lessons in all classrooms and assist with districtwide program implementation (thoughtful use of basal program and/or literature anthology).

4. Offer special program training.
The reading specialist should be a resource for all teachers using programs such as Creating Independence Through Student-Owned Strategies (CRISS), Soar to Success in Reading (SOAR), and Accelerated Reader.

5. Build reading motivation.
The reading specialist should suggest and help implement schoolwide reading incentives.

6. Assist with assessments.
The reading specialist should be available to assess students' reading levels and offer teachers suggestions based on assessment results.

7. Develop parent and community relations.
The reading specialist should be a contact for parent information and assist with parent involvement activities.

These expectations center on using the certified reading specialist as a literacy expert and a literacy resource to the building administrators, all building-level teachers, and parents. Each year, the reading specialist and administrators design the reading specialist's schedule around the needs of the students and teachers, which often requires a great amount of flexibility. This schedule includes working with classroom teachers, modeling lessons, team teaching, observing classrooms or individual students, and collaborative planning with all grade-level teachers. The role of the reading specialist also involves training and supervising paraprofessionals because these individuals often work with small groups of students in need of intervention assistance. Before the school year begins, the reading specialist also attends planning sessions with the school leadership team, and after analysis of the students' content area and reading test scores and literacy portfolios, guides the team in determining the literacy focus for the upcoming school year. This schoolwide planning allows the reading specialist to meet with teachers and design a plan for implementing additional reading and writing strategies with all teachers, in all classrooms, throughout the year. (See chapter 2 for a more detailed explanation of these steps.)

In addition to planning and implementing these focus initiatives, we recommend that the reading specialist assist with individual and group content area and reading assessments, choose and locate material for reading interventions and for reading enrichment, and see small groups of students who need short-term specialized intervention. Each of the reading specialists in my district insists on maintaining the role of providing specialized reading assistance for struggling students because this short-term intervention and assistance has helped many students achieve classroom success, and it helps the reading specialist maintain professional integrity within the school atmosphere. Although meeting with struggling students is important, having the reading specialist scheduled from the first bell to the last bell is not the model designed to assist the most students. With close to 1,000 students in most of the schools in our district, it is impossible to serve the needs of all struggling students. However, as a resource, the reading specialist can be the literacy coach for all the students at the school and touch every child throughout the year in positive literate ways. Coaching teachers while working with students provides a multiplier effect for the reading specialist. If done well and in consensual agreement, the coaching of the reading specialist can raise the skill level of the teacher and raise students' reading abilities as a result ("Coaches, Controversy, Consensus," 2004; "Spotlight on Reading Coaches," 2004; Tatum, 2004).

The Reading Specialist Speaks: Welcome to My World

Becoming the literacy leader in a middle school with more than 1,100 students is something that I never imagined myself doing. However, after spending five years helping to create a school where literacy is a high priority, I cannot imagine myself doing anything else. While completing my master's degree in reading, I predicted that my future would hold a job in an elementary school working with groups of six to eight children and spearheading reading incentives that would encourage children to read. In my experience, that was what the reading specialist did. As a proficient reader in elementary school, I never had the opportunity to work with the reading specialist. He or she would arrive during reading time and whisk away a few students who were in need of assistance. This concept was validated by my experience as a student teacher and an elementary educator for 10 years in schools where the reading specialist provided valuable instruction in a traditional role.

Fortunately for me, the role of the reading specialist has evolved and continues to evolve into something much more challenging, much more demanding, and much more rewarding than what I had visualized. At the middle school where I work, Rodney E. Thompson Middle School, Stafford, Virginia, USA, I am a resource to each and every one of the 1,100 students. At some point in their middle school careers, I have had the opportunity to teach all of them—from the highest achievers to the most challenged learners. I have worked with them not only directly but also indirectly through the training and collaboration that I do with the teachers that they see on a daily basis. I make it a priority to work with the literacy team—all of the staff members in the building— to see that students have reading classes and materials that meet their needs and will help them to improve and enrich their reading.

What does a day in the life of a reading specialist look like due to the evolution that is occurring? It is busy, productive, and definitely diverse. During a typical day I can be found in the computer lab monitoring a reading incentive program, teaching test-taking strategies in an eighth-grade science class, assisting health teachers in designing graphic organizers for use with their curriculum, demonstrating teaching techniques in a seventh-grade reading class, using the social studies curriculum to model active reading strategies for sixth-grade students, collecting and analyzing individual and grade-level test data, providing or preparing for a teacher inservice, or providing small-group assistance for students. While I admit that there are days when a predictable schedule of small-group instruction looks appealing, I am proud to be one of the many reading specialists who, with the support of our supervisors and administrators, is taking the position to a new level—a level that will better meet the needs of students, teachers, and, ultimately, society. A nation of readers and a nation of leaders can only be created through a team effort.

Concluding Remarks

In the following chapters we share suggestions and practical ideas that have worked for us in establishing successful, comprehensive literacy programs at each of our districts' schools. As previously mentioned, the first half of each chapter provides program and administrative suggestions from a supervisor's viewpoint, including supporting research for each component. The second half of each chapter provides multiple examples of practical implementations of the program—which can be adapted to fit an elementary or high school context—that worked for a reading specialist at her assigned middle school.

CHAPTER 2

Developing and Coordinating a Schoolwide Literacy Program

"An effective school reading program must be based upon a broad comprehensive view of reading; it requires a vision of what reading is, and it demands a concerted effort that involves all professionals in the schools working toward a shared vision."

Bean, 2002, p. 4

M OST PROGRESS DOES NOT occur without a clearly articulated vision, followed by careful, thoughtful planning. Designing a comprehensive school literacy program is much like designing a house. There is no one "best" model, although certain best practices or essentials should be present (Lipson, Mosenthal, Mekkelsen, & Russ, 2004; Strickland, Ganske, & Monroe, 2002). A strong commitment to literacy, as evidenced by time allotted every day for reading and writing, appropriate materials, and ongoing staff training, is essential for continued progress for all students. This commitment requires a strong administrator, a knowledgeable reading specialist and/or lead teacher, and supportive staff. Research suggests these components are critical in the study of effective, literate schools (Cunningham & Allington, 1999; Lipson et al., 2004).

Just as the definition of literacy has broadened over time to include a greater degree of skill and ability, so have the responsibilities of the school and the requirements for a schoolwide literacy program. In the past, literacy programs were often designed with the low-performing students in mind. Parent organizations, school boards, and state boards of education all have expressed commitment to this focus on the low-performing reader and writer. Although this is a necessary part of the literacy program, it is only a small part of the entire design. If a school or district focuses only on struggling readers, the struggling readers often never feel as if they are equal, contributing members of the schoolwide literacy community, and the total school population may not progress as it could. Past studies (Allington, 1998; Cunningham & Allington, 1999) suggest that the lower level readers remain struggling literacy students for their entire school career, and often for life, if they do not benefit from a "multifaceted schoolwide approach" (Irvin & Strauss, 2000, p. 117). We have developed a multifaceted model that works for us, and with thoughtful implementation and guidance, the school-based read-

ing specialist can help facilitate the incorporation of this model to promote literacy growth for most students.

The Key Players

Successful schools not only depend on the leadership of key individuals
but also on a strong sense of community and autonomy (Grisham, Lapp,
& Flood, 2000; Lipson et al., 2004; Rasinski & Padak, 2000). A collaborative school community with a high degree of commitment and expectations for all students is characteristic of schools that show positive
literacy results for students. When the reading specialist is given the
opportunity to use his or her expertise to enhance the learning of all students, rather than narrowly focusing on the struggling students, it seems
the results are multiplied in literacy growth for all. In successful schools,
quality teaching is the trademark difference (Cunningham & Allington,
1999; Lipson et al., 2004).

The reading specialist, working through the literacy committee with
the support of the principal, can help all teachers, and thus enhance the
teacher's expertise for each student, every day, in every classroom. The literacy committee is typically composed of teachers and reading specialists in the school building who advise and promote schoolwide literacy.
(See chapter 3 for more information on developing a comprehensive literacy community.) Depending on the level of the school, this committee
may include a representative from each grade level or a representative
from each department in a middle or junior or senior high school. Often,
the media specialist, the music teacher, the art teacher, and a physical education teacher are also members of the literacy committee so that all
content area teachers can assume ownership of students' literacy development. The literacy committee plans and evaluates literacy needs and initiatives for the school, with the reading specialist acting as chairperson of the
committee. To be most effective, the building principal must support the
endeavors of the reading specialist and set the expectation that the reading specialist is a facilitator for everyone in the building.

Crafting a Schoolwide Literacy Vision

As a supervisor, I find it best to begin the school year with a conference with the building administrator to discuss the school's literacy vision, perceived needs, and commitment. (See Table 2.1 for a list of

questions to use in this conference.) I am fortunate to have developed a friendly atmosphere of professional respect with most of the administrators in the school district; however, administrators change at an amazing rate. This year, due to the district's expanding population and retirement of veteran administrators within the district, there are 12 new principals and assistant principals. Consequently, during the summer months or between summer school, meetings, and vacation days, I try to meet with each new principal at least once and get an idea of his or her vision of a comprehensive literacy program for the school. I have ongoing discussions about these topics with seasoned principals.

During the conference, I also share literacy principles of a comprehensive program (see Table 2.2) and discuss how I can help the administrators achieve their goals. These principles include the following:

- Access to a wide range of interesting material
- Instruction that builds the desire and the skill to read
- Assessments that inform the students and the teachers of students' needs and strengths
- Content area teachers who model and apply reading strategies
- Reading specialists and coaches who are available to assist struggling students
- Teachers who understand adolescents' complex literacy needs
- A home–school literacy connection

People often ask me for program recommendations, even to rank the most popular programs as far as each program's effectiveness.

TABLE 2.1
Administrator Discussion Protocol

1. What is your literacy vision for the school?

2. How do you plan to build staff support and enthusiasm for the literacy program?

3. How are you planning the master schedule to help achieve your vision?

4. What are your plans for involving parents in the literacy program?

5. What reading incentives have been successful in your experience?

6. How can I help you achieve your literacy vision for your school?

TABLE 2.2
Suggested Literacy Principles for Planning a Comprehensive School Program

Principles	Examples
Access to a wide range of interesting material.	Arrange a visit by an author of choice. Stock classrooms and media centers with magazines, short novels, and many copies of realistic novels.
Instruction that builds the desire and the skill to read.	Train all teachers in reading strategies. Skilled teachers support vocabulary and comprehension development with daily assistance.
Assessments that inform the students and the teachers of students' needs and strengths.	Use ongoing and student-friendly assessments. Measure reading and writing progress in several ways, including reading logs and writing journals, and incorporate into classroom instruction.
Content area teachers who model and apply reading strategies.	Teachers read aloud daily from engaging informational or fiction texts and share read-aloud think-alouds with students.
Reading specialists and coaches who are available to assist struggling students.	Students come to media center for reading assistance. Reading specialist team teaches with content area teachers and reading teachers. A trained specialist provides before- and after-school tutorials in reading strategies.
Teachers who understand adolescents' complex literacy needs.	Teachers provide adolescents with opportunities to develop reading skills through drama, through computer labs, and by writing and designing literary magazines.
A home–school literacy connection.	The school sends parents newsletters featuring literacy ideas and recommended adolescent literature, invites parents to Homework Help Night to model reading and writing strategies, and provides parents additional copies of classroom novels to read with their children.

Note. Principles provided by Nancy DeVries Guth, Supervisor, Literacy and Humanities, Stafford County Public Schools, Stafford, Virginia, USA.

However, it is impossible to do this without knowing the needs of the teachers, the school, the students, and the community. When we began building our district literacy program, we went through a lot of trial and error. We continue to refine the process every year. The suggestions we offer are based on our experiences and are meant only as a guide as you craft your individual areas of responsibilities. It is imperative to have a well-trained specialist to coordinate these programs in order to maximize their effectiveness. It is much better to invest in a well-trained specialist than a program that may not be used effectively with struggling students or by well-meaning but untrained teachers.

The Reading Specialist Speaks: Setting Up the Program

When I began the position of reading specialist, I had no middle school experience and was helping to establish a new middle school. While it was exciting to begin with a clean slate and have the opportunity to build a program, it was also a little overwhelming. As I began writing this section, I thought to myself, "How did the reading program get to where it is today?" As Nancy mentioned, there was a lot of trial and error, but slowly everything came together. The following suggestions can be used by reading specialists as a guide to help build a reading program (a reference I wish I had when I began building the reading program at my school).

Interview specialists in other buildings and districts.
When I began my position as reading specialist, there were already five middle schools in the county. Each middle school had a reading specialist, so I visited two of them to find out what their programs were like. I found two very busy reading specialists with very different programs. There was consistency in the basic program elements such as time for reading, appropriate materials, instruction that focused on active reading, and incentives that increased motivation; however, each program took on a unique life of its own based on the needs of the staff and students. I used those basic elements as a foundation on which to build my program, and I adapted it as I realized the needs of my particular school population.

If you are in a small school district where there is no other reading specialist in a position similar to the one you are filling, contact other school districts in your area. You can call the district central office to be directed to the necessary contacts. The information that I gathered from those interviews was extremely valuable because it made me realize that every program is unique. The interview protocol in Table 2.3 will be helpful in gathering information about other programs. It

TABLE 2.3
Reading Specialist Interview Protocol

What do you see as your primary responsibilities as a literacy leader?

Schedule

What is your daily schedule?

Do you work with small groups and/or collaborate in the classroom?

How do you schedule small groups?

Do you take students out of a scheduled reading class or from electives?

How long do you work with your groups?

Do you schedule book talks and lessons in the classrooms?

Assessment

What tools do you use to assess students?

    Schoolwide?

    As a group?

    As an individual?

To whom do you report this information?

How do you present this information to the classroom teachers?

How do you use this data to make decisions in your building?

Instruction

Are there specific reading programs that you have used in your building?

Have they been successful? Why or why not?

How are students selected for small-group instruction?

What types of lessons do you use in the classroom?

What types of inservice opportunities do you offer teachers?

How do you assist teachers who are not comfortable with teaching reading?

Motivation

What reading incentives have you used in your building?

Do you have volunteers? How do you effectively use them?

How do you handle rewards?

How do you get funding for incentive rewards?

Resources

Do you have a reading budget?

Are there specific titles that are required or approved for your district?

How are the titles selected?

What companies offer quality materials at a good price?

What type of resources or materials do teachers request the most?

Do you have a resource area set up separate from the media center?

How do teachers check out materials from the resource area?

What do you think is the most rewarding part of your job?

What do you think is the most challenging part of your job?

provides a guideline of questions to ask other reading specialists about their programs. You can use this information as a reference when comparing and contrasting different programs.

Meet with key personnel to discuss the philosophy of the school.
When I was chosen as the reading specialist, a core group of teachers had been hired already and had determined that literacy would be a high priority. They had determined that all sixth- and seventh-grade teachers would be teaching a period of reading and there would be an eighth-grade reading class for those students who did not choose or did not qualify to take a foreign language. Consequently, I realized that I would need many resources available to the sixth- and seventh-grade teachers and that some of them would have little or no experience teaching reading. In addition, several special education teachers expressed concerns about their previous students' experiences with competitive reading incentives, so I knew that some of the incentive ideas I had gathered from other reading specialists would have to be adjusted or abandoned.

Compile a list of what you envision for your program and prioritize it.
After I gathered ideas from other reading specialists and combined it with the information I had from the start-up team, I began to create a framework of what would work for our building. While I initially envisioned myself immediately starting all of these wonderful projects, I soon learned that I had to prioritize and focus on one piece of the literacy puzzle at a time. After one piece was solidly in place, I could add more and build on it. For example, I collaborated with the media specialists on a reading incentive that centered on a state reading initiative, the Virginia Young Readers Program. In one middle school, it had been implemented only in sixth grade and was strictly voluntary, while another middle school used it in seventh grade, and the students were required to read some of the books for class. We decided to make it a voluntary schoolwide incentive, and we focused solely on that incentive for the first year. Once we found a system that worked well for that program, we began to work on our summer reading incentive program. (See chapter 9 for a more detailed description of these programs.) I used the Reading and Resource Evaluation Chart (see Table 2.4) to help determine whether I had the resources, assistance, and funding necessary to implement a

TABLE 2.4

Reading and Resource Evaluation Chart

Program/Incentive	Objective	Target Audience	Time/Management	Resources/Funding/Personnel
Virginia Young Readers Program (see chapter 9)	Motivation	All students	• Book talks—approximately three days per grade level • Time to read and listen to summaries	• 15 copies of 10 titles @ 5.00 each = $750.00 • Pizza Party—approximately $150.00 • Funding—Parent–Teacher Organization and library budget • Reading specialist, media specialists, media center assistant
Recordings for the Blind and Dyslexic (RFBD)—Books on Tape	Instruction	Select special education students and struggling readers	• Train students—one class period for every two to three students • Order and distribute materials • **Provide teachers and paraprofessionals with training in use of materials** • Train a **paraprofessional to distribute tapes to students**	• Talking book machines (purchased with school start-up funds) • RFBD Membership $450.00 per year from special education budget • Reading specialist, **special education teachers, special education paraprofessionals**
National Computer Systems (NCS) Mentor Writing Program	Instruction	All language arts teachers and students	• One day of professional leave for teachers • Half day examining rubric on the computer and half day using rubric to grade student papers and discuss/compare results	• NCS Mentor disc from state department • NCS Mentor trainer from central office • Computer lab • Substitutes
Summer Reading Incentive (see chapter 9)	Motivation	All students	• Revise lists and photocopy—one week • Distribute lists to students and guidance center—one day • Share incentive at student and parent orientations for new students—one hour • Prepare and distribute rewards—one week	• Bookmarks, pencils, treats—$150 • $.25 coupons to school store—$50–$75 • Funding—Parent–Teacher Organization and Reading Budget • Reading specialist, media specialists, media center assistant

Note. This table describes two reading incentives, a reading assistance program and a teacher inservice, that were used in my building. The notations in bold print show how I changed the system to make it more effective.

reading program, incentives, or inservice. It was also an excellent way to evaluate each program and determine if changes could be made to reach more students and use time and resources more effectively. For example, Table 2.4 illustrates two reading incentives, a reading assistance program and a teacher inservice, that were used in my building. After examining the chart, I realized that each year the costs for the Virginia Young Readers Program and the Summer Reading Incentive would rise as more students participated. However, the fact that the participation continued to grow each year also indicated that the programs were successful. After looking at the Books on Tape program, I realized that training all the students and distributing all the materials myself was not an effective use of time and that the instruction was not carrying over into the classroom.

Order trade books and other resources to begin building a resource collection in your classroom or office.
In order to have an effective literacy program, there must be a plethora of resources available to the literacy team. In order for this resource collection to be truly effective, it must be built as the result of a team effort. Coming from an early elementary school position, I had very limited knowledge of which titles and authors were appealing for adolescents. I depended on the assistance of the other reading specialists and the input from the teachers about which books they had used previously, which genre or authors they personally enjoyed, and which books helped reinforce their curricula. During my first few months as a middle school reading specialist, I did a phenomenal amount of reading, which helped me become well versed in the area of adolescent literature and better able to serve as a resource for reading teachers. (See chapter 4 for some basic guidelines for initial ordering and suggestions for building a resource collection that will work for your building.)

Get to know your literacy team.
As a literacy leader, one of the first priorities on your list is to learn the name, grade level, and content area of every staff member in the building. Make yourself a visible and welcoming presence throughout the building. Carefully hone your people skills, such as communicating and listening, so that you can work effectively with all the various personalities in the school environment. (See chapter 3 for a list of simple and practical suggestions for getting to know your team.)

Develop a map for the school year.

I have found that the best way to develop a map for the school year is to use the program model at the beginning of each chapter of this book as a guide. I consider the following questions under each of the responsibilities listed on the model (see chapter 9 for details on motivation):

Leadership

Literacy Program Development and Coordination

- How many teachers are assigned a reading period?
- What reading programs are used in the district or county?
- Is a basal series used?

Staff Development

- What type of staff development has the staff and administration requested?
- What are the best times and days to offer staff development?
- How can I get more than just the reading and language arts teachers to attend?

Resources

- How will teachers request and receive resources?
- How do I make staff members aware of the resources that are available?
- How do I keep track of resources and replace lost or damaged books?

Instruction

Planning and Collaborating With Teachers

- When do the grade levels have planning time?
- How many teachers are assigned a reading period?
- Would teachers prefer to have students pulled out of the classroom or have me come in?

Supporting Classroom Instruction

- What is the curriculum for each subject and grade level?
- What lessons can I present in the classroom that will assist students with testing and content area reading?
- How many teachers are new or have never taught a reading class?

Providing Specialized Support

- What are the criteria for small-group instruction?
- Will students be pulled out of reading class or electives?
- How many groups can I schedule and still be available as a resource?

Diagnosis and Assessment

Administration and Interpretation

- At what grade levels are state or district standardized tests given?
- Are certain diagnostic tools approved or required in the district?
- How will I report the data to the teachers and administration?
- How can I assist the teachers and administration in interpreting the data?
- What diagnostic tools should be used when parents or teachers request testing?

Development and Coordination

- Who will administer the tests?
- How will testing materials be distributed?
- When will testing occur?

After analyzing each area I examine the school year week by week to create a map. Table 2.5 provides an example of my yearly map and clearly illustrates the need for the reading specialist to have a flexible schedule. The map changes throughout the school year and from year to year based on the needs of the staff and students.

Meet with teams or grade levels to discuss how students will be grouped and the goals and curriculum of the reading program.

A strong literacy program requires collaboration, and collaboration requires time to share thoughts and ideas. Over the past five years, we have had a wide variety of reading configurations at Thompson Middle School. My role throughout this time has been to offer guidance, to document what has and has not been successful, and to facilitate change when necessary. I remain open-minded and welcome suggestions and change, but I also am careful to maintain a basic structure of practices that have proven to be successful. (Chapter 6 provides greater detail

TABLE 2.5
Map of School Year

Mo.	Wk.	Reading and Resource Responsibilities	Ongoing Responsibilities			
Aug.	3	Prepare resource area, add new materials, update resource lists	Resource			Staff develop.
	4	New teacher institute	Resource			Staff develop.
Sept.	1	Reading pretest—prepare reports, meet with teams, create groups	Resource		Learning	Staff develop.
	2	Collect Summer Reading Incentive materials	Resource		Strategies	Staff develop.
	3	Active thinking and test-taking strategy lessons in classrooms	Resource		Class	Staff develop.
	4		Resource		2 days	Staff develop.
Oct.	1	Reading strategies lessons—series of three for each class	Resource		per week	Staff develop.
	2		Resource			Staff develop.
	3		Resource		Learning	Staff develop.
	4	Virginia Young Readers (VAYR) Program book talks with media specialists	Resource	VAYR	Strategies	Staff develop.
Nov.	1		Resource	VAYR	Class	Staff develop.
	2	Classroom instruction, content area reading inservice	Resource	VAYR	2 days	Staff develop.
	3	Classroom instruction, content area reading inservice	Resource	VAYR	per week	Staff develop.
	4	Classroom instruction, content area reading inservice	Resource	VAYR		Staff develop.
Dec.	1	Benchmark reading assessment—sixth grade	Resource	VAYR	Learning	Staff develop.
	2	Analyze results, identify specific areas of strength and weakness	Resource	VAYR	Strategies	Staff develop.
	3	Winter break	Resource	VAYR	Class	Staff develop.
	4	Winter break	Resource	VAYR	2 days	Staff develop.
Jan.	1	Specialized groups, classroom instruction	Resource	VAYR	per week	Staff develop.
	2	Specialized groups, classroom instruction	Resource	VAYR		Staff develop.
	3	Specialized groups, classroom instruction	Resource	VAYR	Learning	Staff develop.
	4	Midyear reading check—sixth grade/semester exams	Resource	VAYR	Strategies	Staff develop.

(continued)

TABLE 2.5 (continued)
Map of School Year

Mo.	Wk.	Reading and Resource Responsibilities	Ongoing Responsibilities			
Feb.	1	Specialized groups, classroom instruction	Resource	VAYR	Class	Staff develop.
	2	Specialized groups, classroom instruction	Resource	VAYR	2 days	Staff develop.
	3	Specialized groups, classroom instruction	Resource	VAYR	per week	Staff develop.
	4	Specialized groups, classroom instruction	Resource	VAYR		Staff develop.
Mar.	1	Specialized groups, classroom instruction	Resource		Learning	Staff develop.
	2	Specialized groups, classroom instruction	Resource		Strategies	Staff develop.
	3	Specialized groups, classroom instruction	Resource		Class	Staff develop.
	4	Specialized groups, classroom instruction	Resource		2 days	Staff develop.
Apr.	1	Specialized groups, classroom instruction	Resource		per week	Staff develop.
	2	Specialized groups, classroom instruction	Resource			Staff develop.
	3	Specialized groups, classroom instruction	Resource		Learning	Staff develop.
	4	Specialized groups, classroom instruction	Resource		Strategies	Staff develop.
May	1	Specialized groups, classroom instruction	Resource		Class	Staff develop.
	2	State standardized testing	Resource		2 days	Staff develop.
	3	End of year reading check—sixth grade	Resource		per week	Staff develop.
	4	Collect literacy portfolios, promote Summer Reading Incentive	Resource			Staff develop.
June	1	Reading posttest—all students	Resource		Learning	Staff develop.
	2	Provide test results to teachers and administrators, retrieve and	Resource		Strategies	Staff develop.
	3	inventory resources	Resource		Class	Staff develop.
	4		Resource		2 days	Staff develop.
July		Meet with other specialists to update curriculum, attend conferences	Resource		per week	Staff develop.

Note. The four final columns illustrate ongoing responsibilities that are not limited to a specific period of time.

about how you can plan and collaborate with classroom teachers about the reading program and gives some examples of successful collaborative efforts that I have experienced.)

Listen and learn, and listen and learn some more.
You will receive incredibly valuable information by becoming an expert listener. By listening to the discussions between the other reading specialists at our monthly meetings and listening to the ideas and experiences that the teachers in my building had to offer, I gained information that was not available in any college textbook or through any research study. I learned about programs and incentives that had been implemented in other buildings and why they were or were not successful. I learned about the various assessment tools that had been used, what each of them could help us to learn about a student, and how I could assist the teachers in interpreting the assessment scores. I learned which teachers were excited about teaching reading and which were reluctant, which ones had a multitude of ideas that I could tap into and which were in need of direction. The more I knew about the teachers in my building, the more I was able to help them find a comfortable way to teach reading and the more motivated they became. Finally, I learned that once the three elements essential for success in reading were in place—time for reading, flexible grouping, and appropriate materials—the final element—motivation—could be added so that the potential for student achievement could be greatly increased.

Concluding Remarks

A strong literacy program begins with strong leaders who are able to provide a clear vision of the program and are committed to supporting the vision with time, resources, and examples. Each school has the opportunity to begin every school year by designing or remodeling their school's literacy program to emphasize an aspect of literacy, such as reading, writing, speaking, listening, and visualizing. No one model or plan works for everyone. The exciting challenge is to make the plans fit the needs and the strengths of each school's staff and student body.

CHAPTER 3

Developing a Comprehensive Literacy Community

"Students become readers when they are a part of a community that invites them into the joys of literacy."

Ogle, 2002, p. 59

A NOTHER ASPECT OF THE leadership portion of the literacy program model includes developing a school-based and community-based means of support for the entire literacy focus of the school. First, the school staff needs to develop an understanding of literacy and of the increased literacy requirements of the 21st century. Then, the school staff needs to be nurtured in their understanding that literacy is a schoolwide responsibility.

Dewey (1916/1966) suggests that to be successful, a school must recognize itself as a community life. More recent researchers (Cazden, 1979; Mehan, 1979; Ogle, 2002) remind us that reading is a social activity and very dependent on the social structure of the classroom and the interactions between teacher and peers. Because of the nature of interactions, such as sharing books, opinions, and personal information, classrooms must be places where students feel valued, respected, and safe. Teachers can build community by sharing their own stories and preferences, and the reading specialist can begin by setting the example. What takes place in the classroom, within the daily life of the school, is critical for many students, because it can determine whether or not they become life-long readers (Rasinski & Padak, 2000; Smith, 1997). Teachers and reading specialists can work together to help establish students as honored members of the school literacy community, roles they can enjoy for the rest of their lives. In addition, schoolwide literacy events should be appealing so all students want to participate and join in the literacy community of the school. The top-level administrator, often deferring to the reading specialist as the energizing source, must support the collective energy of a school community to foster literacy within the daily life of the school. Moore (2000) suggests that it is imperative to give attention to contextual issues, such as administrative support, resource availability, and parent support, when establishing a literacy community, all of which are important aspects of a successful literacy program.

Teachers Administrators

Resources → Parents

Planning and Collaborating With Teachers

Staff Development

Supporting Classroom Instruction

Literacy Program Development and Coordination

Providing Specialized Support

leadership — instruction

motivation

diagnosis and assessment

Administration and Interpretation

Development and Coordination

Literacy Community Hierarchy

As illustrated in Figure 3.1, the literacy community includes the entire school district—all community members, students, parents, support staff, teachers, and administrators. Each community has expectations for literacy performance and literacy participation, and expects the school to support these expectations. The school literacy team is the next level. The

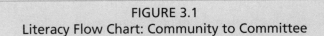

FIGURE 3.1
Literacy Flow Chart: Community to Committee

The Literacy Community
Students, parents, school board, central office personnel, administrators, reading specialist, media specialist, teachers, paraprofessionals, support staff, and community members
Responsibilities: Provide suggestions and support for literacy-related events and instruction

---

The School Literacy Team
Administrators, reading specialist, media specialist, teachers, paraprofessionals, and support staff
Responsibilities: Provide instruction and support for literacy within the school day

---

The School Literacy Committee
Administrative designee, reading specialist, media specialist, grade-level representative, and other specialists representative(s) *
Responsibilities: Implement and support daily literacy instruction within the school context

---

The District Literacy Committee
Supervisor, reading specialists, and key building representatives from each schoolwide committee
Responsibilities: Formulate policies and make suggestions for each school community

---

* May include English as a second language (ESL) teachers; special education teachers; art, music, and drama teachers.

school literacy team consists of every teacher and administrator in the school—from the physical education department to foreign language and from technology to fine arts—and includes the paraprofessionals and all reading specialists. The third level of the literacy flowchart is the school literacy committee. The members of this committee can vary according to the expertise of the staff and the needs of the school. Usually the committee includes a representative from each grade level as well as specialists such as music teachers and media specialists. The responsibilities of the school literacy committee are more specific and directly related to all aspects of literacy instruction, including language arts/reading and writing, in an effort to fulfill the needs and expectations of the community and school. The district literacy committee includes supervisors, reading specialists, and representatives from each school literacy committee. The responsibilities of this committee include formulating procedures and making suggestions for each school community.

Literacy issues may originate and flow in either direction. Literacy issues—for example, the use of a particular trade book for instruction—may originate from a parent (i.e., the literacy community), a teacher (i.e., the school literacy committee), or the central office (i.e., the district literacy committee). The school literacy committee is responsible for maintaining the flow of communication for school concerns to the school district and thus receives guidance and support for literacy issues and needs. This may include conference attendance for teachers, training—site based or district based—material recommendations and purchases, or use of a new trade book.

Working With Your School Literacy Committee

As explained in chapter 2, the building administrator is the instructional leader as well as the primary literacy leader and supporter for the school. After the building administrator and the central office representative together establish the literacy vision for the building, the administrator is responsible for developing a school-level literacy committee, with the reading specialist as a chairperson of the committee. Principals often select a strong teacher from each grade level or select an English/reading teacher from each grade-level team to be on the committee, depending on the size and management style of the school. The administrator should also be an active, participating member of the team, although the degree of participation depends on the size of the school and the background and expertise of the administrator. Some of our administrators choose to attend every meeting of the school literacy committee, guiding the focus, while others choose to supervise with suggestions and maintain a supportive, behind-the-scenes role. At the elementary level, a respected teacher at each grade level can be chosen to be on the committee, in addition to the media specialist. At the middle level, each grade level and each specialist area (e.g., physical education, fine arts) should be represented. This way, every teacher in the school will feel they have a voice in the committee. Several representatives from the school literacy committee also attend the district literacy committee meetings, where district-level issues are discussed and resolved. It is necessary to have an organizational hierarchy (see Figure 3.1 on page 29) but also to have everyone feel as if they have an opportunity to be heard.

At the elementary, middle, or high school level, it is equally important to create an aura of acceptance and enjoyment around the act of reading. Reading must be seen as a part of everyday life and every content area. The school literacy committee should keep reading at the forefront of school life. There is a place in every classroom for pleasure reading and that pleasure must be regularly highlighted by all school staff to entice students into the world of reading for pleasure. The school literacy committee should suggest activities to highlight reading, consistently recognize readers for achievements in reading, and continually update classroom reading materials so students see reading as relevant and enticing. Because many students arrive at school with thousands of hours of wonderful literacy experiences while others have had no warm personal experiences at home or perhaps in previous school experience (Ogle, 2002), the school literacy committee must provide these experiences for all students throughout the school year.

Supporting Your School Literacy Committee

The reading specialist needs the support of the school's teachers, administrators, and parents in order to lead a school community in fostering literacy growth. It may be a daunting task, but starting with one teacher, one willing grade level, and one group of parents is often the best way to lead others. If one teacher comments positively on a lesson the reading specialist shared or a book the reading specialist recommended, or a student remarks publicly about the books he or she is reading from the reading resource room, then the interest grows in having the reading specialist work as a partner with others. The magic of placing the right book in the hand of the teacher, and then showing the teacher how to enjoy the book with his or her students, is often the spark that ignites the literacy enjoyment and involvement for students.

This cycle also is true with parents. When one parent has a positive experience with a book, a reading strategy, or a writing assignment, he or she is able to touch other parents with the positive experience. The simple act of asking a parent to come into school and read a book to a class or help the teacher with an editing lesson—or even inviting parents to a breakfast buddies program—can stimulate a positive experience for parents and help them realize the importance of reading and writing in and out of school.

For example, one school in our district wanted to make positive community connections and initiate community literacy involvement, so the school designated Dr. Seuss's birthday as Community Reading Day and invited all parents and all the nearby businesses—through an employee or representative—to come into school and share a favorite book or other reading. Parents signed up with their child's teacher, or if individuals did not have a child in the school, they could sign up with the reading specialist. The reading specialist and the media specialist had a table with treats, name tags, and many book selections set up in the front lobby the entire day. Businesses donated coffee, juice, cookies, and donuts, and many community workers stopped in to see the school, read to a class, and establish a positive connection—many of which continue to develop. It was such a success that the school chose to make Community Reading Day an annual affair. The event was even recognized in the International Reading Association's journal *The Reading Teacher* (Guth, 2002).

The Reading Specialist Speaks: Getting Everyone Involved as a Member of the Literacy Community

As a literacy leader, I quickly became aware of the many individuals who are a part of the literacy community and realized that I needed to find a way to interact with all of them. Although the students and the teachers assigned to a reading class were obvious priorities, I needed to reach out to the rest of the community to ensure a successful literacy program because when students understand and appreciate that literacy is a part of everyday life in the real world, they are able to get the most out of school-based literacy activities.

It is imperative that the members of the literacy committee (every staff member in the building) know who the reading specialist is, what resources are available, where the resources are located, and how to check out resources. In addition, the reading specialist must know the literacy team—their names, grade levels, content areas, interests, and attitudes about literacy. Parents also should be able to recognize the reading specialist and should understand that this individual is a resource for everyone. Reading specialists have to be a visible and welcoming presence for parents, in addition to the teachers in their building. Following are some ideas reading specialists can use to get to know the literacy team, reach out to parents, and ensure administrators are involved in the literacy program:

Set a positive tone from the beginning of the school year.
At the first faculty meeting, introduce yourself and share some of the resources that are available, but keep it brief because teachers are overwhelmed at this point. They simply need to know who you are, where you are, and what services you can provide.

Create a reading display for Open House.
Take a photograph of each staff member preparing his or her classroom or reading a book (which gives you an opportunity to put names and faces together). Or request that each staff member have a picture taken while reading at home or while on vacation over the summer. Post the photographs on a display for Open House.

Send out the message that staff members are readers.
Set up a database with the name of each staff member in your building. Don't forget to include paraprofessionals, itinerant teachers, custodians, and cafeteria staff. Create signs to be posted outside each classroom or office door that says, "Mr. Smith is currently reading...." Mount the sign on a piece of construction paper and laminate it. Personally deliver each sign and ask staff members to help promote reading by posting the sign outside their classroom doors and updating the sign by adding what they are currently reading.

Tap into the knowledge of the educators in your building.
Have teachers complete an informal survey providing information about the experiences that they have had in other buildings, what reading programs have or have not been effective, what types of staff development

they would like to have, what titles or resources they would like to have available in the resource room, and what particular genre or authors they personally enjoy teaching. Asking for their input and making sure that you act on it is important because it sends the message that this is "our program" not "my program."

Build a resource area in your classroom or office and be available to offer guidance to teachers looking for materials or ideas.
Walking into a room full of classroom sets of novels can be confusing and intimidating for teachers who are unfamiliar with adolescent literature. Be available to guide teachers to books or materials that will work for them based on the reading level of their students, their students' interests, and the teachers' interests. As you plan your weekly schedule, leave opportunities for each grade level to visit during their planning time. For example, the sixth-grade teachers in my building have second and third period as their planning time. I also know that seventh-grade teachers need time available during fourth and fifth period because these are their planning periods and that eighth-grade teachers will likely need me at the end of the school day because that is when they have their planning periods. Therefore, when I plan my weekly or monthly schedule I make sure that I leave open some time during these periods so that I am available as a resource.

In addition, compile a list of resources and trade books available in the resource area and personally distribute it. Share resources such as *Kids Discover, Current Science, Current Health*, or local educational periodicals with content area teachers—not just teachers teaching a reading class. Also share content area resource books or activities that might help reinforce teachers' curricula.

Volunteer for an ongoing position.
Volunteering will keep you informed about what is happening in the school and will encourage staff members to communicate with you. The position that I have found to be really effective is to be the contact person for the local paper. Not only does it give me the opportunity to interact with staff members who I may not see on a regular basis, but also it keeps me abreast of what is happening in our building. In addition, I serve on a leadership committee, a group that meets biweekly to discuss staff concerns, upcoming events, and how to improve the effectiveness of the instructional programs within our building.

Follow up on materials that you have provided.

Remember to check with teachers to see how their units are going, how the students are reacting to books, and to remind them that if they need anything, you are available. Ask teachers if the resource materials you have provided are working or if they would like you to look for additional materials. Offer to demonstrate teaching techniques in their classrooms.

Provide staff development opportunities within your building.

After the needs of the staff have been determined, work with administrators to develop opportunities that will be meaningful and convenient for the staff. Administrative support for the reading program has allowed me the opportunity to provide the staff at my school with inservice opportunities that have increased the effectiveness of instruction in all content and elective courses. As part of our school improvement plan, all staff members were required to attend a content area reading class. Rather than have teachers attend training after school, I received permission to provide the training during the school day. I led the training, along with a seventh-grade language arts, reading, and civics teacher, and it was well received. Optimal learning occurred because the staff was not tired or worried about getting home late; they seemed to feel that their personal time was being taken into consideration. The training also provided an opportunity for staff members who were not familiar with each other to get together. Having every member of the literacy team from the physical education department to the foreign language department in these classes also allowed us to develop a common vocabulary to use throughout the curricular areas. For example, when a physical education teacher told the students that they would be taking notes on a two-column chart or using a Venn diagram, the students were familiar with the terms and could easily follow the teacher's instruction. Consequently, each year this opportunity is provided for new teachers. This past school year, a seventh-grade math and reading teacher and a sixth-grade language arts and reading teacher assisted in the training. Having teachers from various curricular areas lead the training has significantly increased the information and examples that can be provided to the participants. It also provides additional resources for new teachers—people they may rely on for assistance or even observe in the classroom. (See Table 3.1 for examples of other staff development activities that you can offer teachers in your building.)

When you offer a staff development activity, create a sign-up sheet and post it in an area that almost everyone comes through on a daily basis (such as the door of the faculty restroom). Send an e-mail to staff

TABLE 3.1
Examples of Staff Development Opportunities

Title	Target Audience	Objectives	Materials	Time Frame
Content Area Reading Strategies to Promote Active Learning	All teachers	Provide teachers with strategies to help their students become active, independent learners	Packet of materials or manual that includes all information covered in the class	Approximately 10–12 hours
Planning Active Learning Activities Using Content Area Reading Strategies	Teachers who have successfully completed the content area training class	Allow teachers the opportunity to plan lessons with other content area teachers and to create activities to use in their classroom	Materials or manual from content class, markers, transparencies, notecards, folders, access to photocopy machine	Approximately 5 hours
Teachers as Readers: Introduction to the Virginia Young Readers Program	All teachers	Provide participants with an overview of the program from the state to the school level, familiarize them with each of the selected titles, and allow them to work independently to create a poster to promote the program	Copies of each of the books being used in the program	Approximately 5 hours 1 hour of instruction and 4 hours of independent work

(continued)

36

Title	Target Audience	Objectives	Materials	Time Frame
Help! I'm Teaching Reading!	All teachers assigned to a reading class	Demonstrate a variety of ways to teach reading using novels, newspapers, and other resources Provide basic information about the reading process and specific vocabulary that is used schoolwide when instructing students in active reading strategies	Novels, novel units, newspapers, graphic organizers, and any other materials utilized by the instructor	Approximately 10 hours 5 hours of instruction and 5 hours of peer observation
Examining and Understanding Reading Assessments	All teachers and administrators involved in testing	Allow teachers time to examine and discuss the reading assessments used in the building; provide specifics as to what information can be gained from each test; and clarify commonly used terms, such as independent and instructional reading level, decoding skills, and so forth	Copies of assessments, access to computers, examples of anonymous student test results	Approximately 5 hours
National Computer Systems (NCS) Mentor Writing Program	All language arts teachers	Provide teachers with the rubric used by the state to assess student writing; allow them the opportunity to read and score actual papers and compare their results with those of the state, and to do the same with papers from their classes	NCS mentor disc from the state department, NCS mentor trainer, and access to computers	Approximately 5 hours 3 hours of instruction, 2 hours to score and compare student papers

members to give them the information about the staff development activity and the location of the sign-up sheet. If your school uses an online system for registration and tracking professional development, be sure to get your activity posted online and offer assistance to those unfamiliar with accessing the program.

Offer a mini-inservice for one hour before or after school.
Often teachers have difficulty setting aside a three- to five-hour period of time to attend staff development. One option I use to overcome this obstacle is to create a menu of one-hour sessions from which teachers can select a class. The sessions might include a review of new materials in the resource room, a quick lesson on reading strategies, a review of different assessment materials, and so forth. Figure 3.2 is an example of a staff development menu of mini-inservice classes that I created and posted in a common area to advertise these sessions. Additional spaces can be added for teachers to sign up, if needed. Often these short sessions work as infomercials that encourage teachers to sign up for some of the staff development opportunities outlined in Table 3.1. Additional session topics could include examining reading assessments, interpreting reading assessments, understanding and using graphic organizers for content area comprehension, an introduction to a reading incentive, or a make-and-take session for creating hands-on materials to share with others.

Invite parents to become active members of the literacy community.
In order to quickly dispel the preconceived notion that the reading specialist is only a resource for reluctant readers, I make sure that I speak to parents at orientations for upcoming sixth graders and other students new to our building. I discuss the summer reading incentive and the Virginia Young Readers Program (detailed in chapter 9) and talk about what a wonderful reading program their students will become a part of. I invite parents to volunteer in the resource room or the media center and encourage them to read with their children.

I also make sure that I am in the halls to speak with parents (and help them locate classrooms) during open house, back-to-school night, and conference nights.

Plan learning opportunities for parents.
Parents are valuable members of the literacy community and their support strengthens our efforts as educators; therefore, after staff members

FIGURE 3.2
Sample Listing of Mini-Inservice Lessons

How About a Quickie?

These one-hour sessions are designed to provide you with some great information in a way that fits your busy schedule! Each class will be held from 3:15 to 4:15 in the reading resource room (146) or the computer lab. You will need to sign up for a minimum of three hours. If you have ideas for other sessions, please let me know. Hope to see you at some of the classes.

Help! I'm Teaching Reading!

Are you a first-time reading teacher? Do you need some ideas for getting a novel unit or reading project started? Come to this session for some practical, easy-to-implement ideas that will make teaching reading enjoyable for you and your students. (Room 146)

Tuesday, September 10   or   Thursday, September 12

_____   _____

_____   _____

Reading Resource Review

We have some great new materials and novels in the resource room this year! Spend an hour reviewing the materials and discussing how you can use them to strengthen your curriculum. (Room 146)

Tuesday, September 17   Wednesday, September 18   Thursday, September 19
Sixth Grade   Seventh Grade   Eighth Grade

_____   _____   _____

_____   _____   _____

Preparing the Literacy Portfolio

Not sure what to put in the portfolio? Wondering exactly how to fill out the information on the cover? Need ideas for helping students keep an independent reading log? Bring your portfolio and your roll sheet with the names and birth dates of your students and we'll work on them together! (Room 146)

Monday, September 22   or   Wednesday, September 24

_____   _____

_____   _____

Computerized Reading Support

Is there anything available in the computer lab to assess students, build reading skills, and provide reading motivation? You bet there is! Visit the sixth-grade computer lab (Room 121) to find out what is available for you and your students.

Monday, September 29   or   Thursday, October 2

_____   _____

_____   _____

have completed the content area reading classes, I offer parents the opportunity to attend a similar class. Many of the strategies that the staff members learned and that are being used in classrooms are demonstrated and discussed during this training. Parents are provided with the opportunity to learn about different ways to help their children become active readers, organize information through effective note-taking and graphic organizers, and study. I was thrilled with parents' enthusiasm after the first training session—so many of them wanted to help their children succeed, but they simply did not know how to help them. As a literacy leader, I realized that staff development did not end with the faculty in my building. It included reaching out to the parents who are a vital part of the literacy community.

Allow your administrators the opportunity to show their support. I make it a priority to invite administrators to attend staff development activities, book talks, special presentations, or to visit while I am doing reading lessons throughout the building. For example, during the content area reading class I presented for teachers, the principal was an active participant during the entire two days of training. The superintendent and assistant superintendent also visited during one of the training days, and the supervisor of reading showed up, participated, and offered her support during the teacher and parent workshops. Why did they come? They came because they were invited. I sent them e-mails, called them, sent reminders, and personally visited them to remind them to stop by if they had a few moments. As a reading specialist I recommend being relentless in your invitations because I have found from experience that the presence of an administrator adds an increased level of validity to any activity. In addition, it allows you the opportunity to demonstrate your skills and abilities as a literacy leader.

Concluding Remarks

The challenge in creating a successful schoolwide literacy program is the implementation, which depends on support from the key players. When all educators feel valued and included and take ownership in the literacy plan, they experience a sense of efficacy, which, in turn, helps create a positive atmosphere for everyone involved.

CHAPTER 4

Building an Effective Resource Collection

"These thoughts provide clear direction. Students need to be given time to read, provided with an assortment of reading materials from which to choose, asked to do few answer-the-questions-in-the-packet assignments, and offered trade books rather than reading or literature anthologies."

Lowery-Moore, 1998, p. 33

ANOTHER COMPONENT OF THE leadership portion of the literacy program model is resources. When teachers have the resources and opportunities to create conditions that foster independent reading, students will read and the entire school literacy program will flourish. Through their leadership efforts, reading specialists can help their schools build a collection of appropriate reading materials so that reading can be seen as an interesting and valuable way to spend instructional time, as well as free time. By creating the means to read, specialists can help stimulate students' desire to read and thus become part of a respected school literacy community.

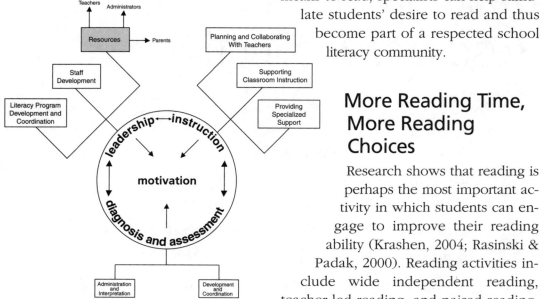

More Reading Time, More Reading Choices

Research shows that reading is perhaps the most important activity in which students can engage to improve their reading ability (Krashen, 2004; Rasinski & Padak, 2000). Reading activities include wide independent reading, teacher-led reading, and paired reading. By matching books to students' interests and abilities, students' time spent reading will increase. When resources are available to make reading a pleasurable and interesting pastime, even reluctant readers will join the literacy team. The reality in most U.S. elementary schools today is that most students do achieve approximate grade-level reading ability by the end of third grade, but students who continue to struggle often remain below grade-level readers throughout their educational careers (Mueller, 2001; Tompkins, 2001). As the demands for higher-level literacy skills have increased, students' reading skills have not kept up with the demands. I believe, and research indicates, that this is a literacy crisis, but it is a crisis of aliteracy rather than illiteracy—that is, students choose not to read instead of not being able to read (Beers, 1998, 2003; Irvin & Strauss, 2000; Krashen, 2004). Therefore, reading specialists must provide books that engage as well as teach, that enthrall as well as educate. Kasten and Wilfong (2005) ascertain that educators have a responsibility to teach students to want to read, which they suggest is more challenging than teaching students how to read. To meet state and national requirements, students must be able to read with comprehension at levels higher than ever before (O'Neal & Kapinus, 2000). However, state and national curriculum standards are totally unattainable if the students cannot read and comprehend the required material. Resources must be plentiful and at students' reading and interest levels to develop the kind of reading skills that students need to be successful in the world today. Consequently, reading specialists must have the knowledge to suggest books to teachers, students, and parents.

An active and informed school literacy committee has the potential to assist struggling readers by ensuring that they have the opportunity to read material (e.g., books, magazines, texts) on their instructional level and on their interest level throughout the school day. Over the course of a school year, we have seen students' reading scores increase from a third- or fourth-grade level to sixth- or seventh-grade level, as measured by informal reading inventories. In our experience, the students who made the most progress were those who had a scheduled reading time during the school day in addition to an English or language arts class. Due to the support of the school literacy committee and assistance of the reading specialists at each school, teachers were able to provide students with a variety of reading materials in each content area.

Organizing Resources for Choice and Voice

When teachers walk into the reading specialist's resource room, they are immediately enticed by the wide variety of books, magazines, and other teaching resources. But it is not chaotic. The books are carefully labeled by appropriate grade level, subject area, and suggested program (e.g., Virginia Young Readers reading promotion). Teachers are busy people with many responsibilities. It has been our experience that if a teacher has to hunt for a particular book or go to the library for a title that relates to his or her subject area, he or she may not always follow through with the task. However, if a teacher can fill out a slip of paper and put it in the reading specialist's mailbox or walk to the resource room at planning time, the task can be accomplished more readily.

A great deal of planning and attention to detail is imperative to the success of any literacy program. With the additional consideration of state and federal mandates, curriculum requirements, and parental pressure, it is essential to take time before each school year to thoughtfully assess the needs of the students and staff. Schools' successes in the area of literacy achievement do not happen by accident, and ample financial resources do not guarantee them. Successful schools seem to be characterized by thoughtful educators who carefully plan for schoolwide success (Lipson, Mosenthal, Mekkelsen, & Russ, 2004). It is necessary to consider the personal preferences of the readers and the teachers while planning for the year. It is also imperative to foster motivation developed by situational interest (Schiefele, 1991), such as desire to participate in the classroom proceedings related to book talks, discussions, and other literacy events built into the school culture. Through the reading specialist's efforts such as building a resource collection and fostering motivation, students will be more likely to pick up and read material that they believe is interesting and relevant to their lives; thus, students will read more often.

Our program began slowly, by organizing a few trade books to complement the core basal and literature anthology. Every year we add book titles that relate to the periods of study in curricular areas, as well as teacher-, parent-, student-, or library-recommended titles. Because we work in a public school system, we carefully evaluate each and every book to ensure that it is not offensive in a cultural or religious sense. The teacher or reading specialist who suggests the book is responsible for writing a rationale for using the book. Rationales are kept in notebooks at each school site and at the district central office. (See Figure 4.1 for a sample rationale.) We started with one small notebook and have progressed to a notebook for each grade level. However, rationales are required only for the class-shared titles—that is, titles read by the entire class although at students' individual rates. If a title is used for independent reading and is a free-choice title, a rationale is not required. If a parent has an objection to a title, students are allowed to read an alternative title. With these guidelines in place, we only receive about one objection a year, and it can be resolved immediately.

The Reading Specialist Speaks: Acquiring the Resources to Support the Program

I am proud of the resources that are available to promote and improve literacy in our building. Although I wish I could take credit for all of them, I cannot. We have built our resource collection based on the

FIGURE 4.1
Rationale Form for Acquisition of Trade Books or Other Supplementary Reading Material

DATE: _____

TEACHER: _____ SCHOOL: _____

TITLE: _____

AUTHOR: _____

GRADE OR COURSE: _____

CRITERIA FOR SELECTION
- contribution the reading material makes to the curriculum
- contribution the reading material makes to the interests of the students
- favorable reviews found in standard selection sources
- professional repute and significance of the author
- contribution the material makes to a variety of viewpoints and issues
- quality of writing
- cost commensurate with need and usage
- timeliness or permanence
- accuracy and validity
- readability
- contribution of the material to increasing the breadth and depth of material available on races, cultures, and religions found in the community

Objectives for lesson or unit:
_____
_____

Ways in which the book is especially appropriate for students in this class:
_____
_____

Ways in which the book is especially pertinent to the objectives of this course/unit:
_____
_____

Is the book currently read at another grade level? _____

Special problems that might arise in relation to the book and your response in addressing this situation: (Please consider the following: witchcraft and the occult, racism and sexism, politics, profanity, sex and sexuality, secular humanism, creationism, and Family Life "opt-out topics.")
_____
_____

Some other appropriate books student might read in place of this book:
_____
_____

Teacher's signature: _____ Date:_____

Principal's signature: _____ Date:_____

Please allow sufficient time for your request to be considered.

From Stafford County Public Schools English Curriculum (2004).

requests and suggestions of the literacy team that, as previously mentioned, includes every teacher in the building. In addition, the constant networking with the other building reading specialists in the district helps provide the opportunity to discuss new materials or programs that are working in other buildings. Just as reciprocal teaching is an effective strategy for our teachers, *reciprocal resourcing* is an effective strategy for building a collection of resources that will meet the needs of all the teachers and students in your building. Reading specialists can use the following criteria as they search for new resources.

Consult the districtwide list of approved trade books.

If a list of approved trade books does not exist in your district, form a committee of reading specialists and teachers to create one. All books included on the list should have a detailed rationale (see Figure 4.1, page 47), which includes a summary of the book and its correlation to the district and state standards. It should also list any content or language that may raise objections to the book (e.g., profanity, violence) and include suggestions for alternative titles. The rationale should be completed by the teacher requesting to use the book and approved by the reading specialist and the building principal. Figures 4.2 and 4.3 are examples of completed rationale forms. In each building, maintain a binder of rationales for the books on the list for easy reference.

Correlate materials with curriculum and state standards.

Be aware of what is being taught in all content areas at all grade levels in order to select trade books and materials that will reinforce the curriculum. Table 4.1 provides a list of book titles that I have found effective in reinforcing the middle school curriculum in my school.

As the curriculum changes, make the necessary adjustments on the trade book list. For example, in my school, the U.S. Civil War was covered in sixth grade so there were a large number of historical fiction titles from that era on the sixth-grade reading list. Then, the curriculum changed and the Civil War was covered in fifth grade, so the trade book list had to be revised. Another example is when I realized that I had 120 copies of *Shades of Gray* (Reeder, 1989) taking up shelf space. I kept enough for a class set and shipped the rest to the reading specialist at the elementary school so that she could add the books to her resource area to support her curriculum.

FIGURE 4.2
Completed Rationale Form for Acquisition of Trade Books or Other Supplementary Reading Material

DATE: _November 15, 2001_

TEACHER: _All Middle School Teachers_   SCHOOL: _Stafford County Public Schools_

TITLE: _Harry Potter and the Sorcerer's Stone (and series)_

AUTHOR: _JK Rowling_

GRADE OR COURSE: _Middle school reading, middle school English/language arts_

CRITERIA FOR SELECTION

- contribution the reading material makes to the curriculum
- contribution the reading material makes to the interests of the students
- favorable reviews found in standard selection sources
- professional repute and significance of the author
- contribution the material makes to a variety of viewpoints and issues
- quality of writing
- cost commensurate with need and usage
- timeliness or permanence
- accuracy and validity
- readability
- contribution of the material to increasing the breadth and depth of material available on races, cultures, and religions found in the community

Objectives for lesson or unit:

English Standard of Learning (SOL) 6.3, 6.4, 6.6

English SOL 74, 75, 77

English SOL 82, 83, 85

The story emphasizes descriptive language and builds vivid vocabulary knowledge through the use of imagery, invented words, and dialect.

Ways in which the book is especially appropriate for students in this class:

The book's plot and characters are very high interest to adolescents. The story line is familiar and is an opportunity to compare and evaluate actual plot with media hype.

Ways in which the book is especially pertinent to the objectives of this course/unit:

The book(s) provide excellent examples of fantasy fiction; the author's craft in the use of word choice, imagery, and invented words develop the students' vocabulary.

Is the book currently read at another grade level? _6th, 7th, or 8th, as determined by each middle school_

Special problems that might arise in relation to the book and your response in addressing this situation: (Please consider the following: witchcraft and the occult, racism and sexism, politics, profanity, sex and sexuality, secular humanism, creationism, and Family Life "opt-out topics.")

The book mentions witchcraft, fantasy, wizards, trolls as part of the mystical fantasy theme.

Some other appropriate books student might read in place of this book:

Ella Enchanted by GC Levine (1997), Just Ella by MP Haddix (1999),
The Witch of Blackbird Pond by E.G. Speare (1989)

Teacher's signature: _____   Date: _____

Principal's signature: _____   Date: _____

Please allow sufficient time for your request to be considered.

DATE: _October 26, 1999_

TEACHER: _Seventh Grade Teachers_   SCHOOL: _Stafford County Public Schools_

TITLE: _Holes_

AUTHOR: _Louis Sachar_

GRADE OR COURSE: _Seventh Grade English_

CRITERIA FOR SELECTION

- contribution the reading material makes to the curriculum
- contribution the reading material makes to the interests of the students
- favorable reviews found in standard selection sources
- professional repute and significance of the author
- contribution the material makes to a variety of viewpoints and issues
- quality of writing
- cost commensurate with need and usage
- timeliness or permanence
- accuracy and validity
- readability
- contribution of the material to increasing the breadth and depth of material available on races, cultures, and religions found in the community

Objectives for lesson or unit:

Plot development, characterization, predicting, inferences, and vocabulary will all be objectives
The book will also be tied in to civics and legal issues.

Ways in which the book is especially appropriate for students in this class:

The circumstances surrounding the main character's incarceration are believable
and are easily understood. The dialogue and actions and thoughts are appropriate for
seventh-grade students. Also, the book lends itself to predicting and interpreting at an
individual level.

Ways in which the book is especially pertinent to the objectives of this course/unit:

This book lends itself to the objectives of predicting because the author purposefully makes
the reader wonder about particular behaviors of characters. It is also an excellent book to
use for oral language in discussions.

Is the book currently read at another grade level? _No_

Special problems that might arise in relation to the book and your response in addressing this situation: (Please consider the following: witchcraft and the occult, racism and sexism, politics, profanity, sex and sexuality, secular humanism, creationism, and Family Life "opt-out topics.")

"curse" of the grandfather

Some other appropriate books student might read in place of this book:

Chernowitz by F. Arrick (1981)

Nothing But the Truth by Avi (2003)

Teacher's signature: _____   Date:_____

Principal's signature: _____   Date:_____

Please allow sufficient time for your request to be considered.

From Stafford County Public Schools English Curriculum (2004).

TABLE 4.1
Trade Books That Reinforce the Curriculum

Westward Movement

Yep, L. (1993). *Dragon's gate*. New York: HarperCollins.

Karr, K. (1998). *The great turkey walk*. New York: Farrar Straus Giroux.

Gipson, F. (2001). *Old Yeller*. New York: Perennial Classics. (Original work published 1956)

Woodruff, E. (1994). *Dear Levi: Letters from the Overland Trail*. New York: Knopf.

Osborne, M.P. (1999). *Buffalo before breakfast*. New York: Random House.

U.S. Civil War

Hunt, I. (1993). *Across five Aprils*. Morristown, NJ: Silver Burdett Press.

Reeder, C. (1989). *Shades of gray*. New York: Macmillan.

Lyons, M.E., & Branch, M. (2000). *Dear Ellen Bee*. New York: Atheneum.

Fleischman, P. (1993). *Bull Run*. New York: HarperCollins.

Stolz, M. (1997). *A ballad of the Civil War*. New York: HarperCollins.

Banks, S.H. (1999). *Abraham's battle: A novel of Gettysburg*. New York: Atheneum.

Osborne, M.P. (2000). *Civil War on Sunday*. New York: Random House.

Polacco, P. (1994). *Pink and Say*. New York: Philomel.

Word War I

Lawrence, I. (2001). *Lord of the Nutcracker men*. New York: Delacorte Press.

Ingold, J. (1998). *Pictures, 1918*. San Diego, CA: Harcourt Brace.

North, S. (1990). *Rascal*. New York: Puffin.

Great Depression

Ryan, P.M. (2000). *Esperanza rising*. New York: Scholastic.

Stanley, J. (1992). *Children of the Dust Bowl: The true story of the school at Weedpatch Camp*. New York: Crown.

Peck, R. (1998). *A long way from Chicago*. New York: Dial Books for Young Readers.

Hesse, K. (1997). *Out of the dust*. New York: Scholastic.

Curtis, C.P. (1999). *Bud, not Buddy*. New York: Delacorte Press.

Taylor, M.D. (1990). *Mississippi Bridge*. New York: Dial Books for Young Readers.

Immigration to the United States

Hesse, K. (1993). *Letters from Rifka*. New York: Puffin.

Woodruff, E. (1997). *The Orphan of Ellis Island: A time travel adventure*. New York: Scholastic.

Tanaka, S. (1996). *On board the Titanic: What it was like when the great liner sank*. New York: Hyperion.

Osborne, M.P. (1999). *Tonight on the Titanic*. New York: Random House.

Bunting, E. (1999). *Dreaming of America: An Ellis Island story*. Mahwah, NJ: Bridge Water Books.

World War II

Yolen, J. (1990). *The devil's arithmetic*. New York: Puffin.

Lisle, J.T. (2000). *The art of keeping cool*. New York: Atheneum.

Wolff, V.E. (1998). *Bat 6*. New York: Scholastic.

Avi. (2001). *Don't you know there's a war going on?* New York: HarperCollins.

Reiss, J. (1972). *The upstairs room*. New York: Crowell.

Schnur, S. (1994). *The shadow children*. New York: William Morrow.

Giff, P.R. (1997). *Lily's crossing*. New York: Delacorte Press.

Lowry, L. (1989). *Number the stars*. Boston: Houghton Mifflin.

(continued)

TABLE 4.1 (continued)
Trade Books That Reinforce the Curriculum

French, J. (2003). *Hitler's daughter*. New York: HarperCollins.
Bishop, C.H. (1978). *Twenty and ten*. New York: Puffin.
Coerr, E. (1977). *Sadako and the thousand paper cranes*. New York: Puffin.
Yep, L. (1995). *Hiroshima: A novella*. New York: Scholastic.
Polacco, P. (2000). *The butterfly*. New York: Philomel.

Civil Rights Movement
Robinet, H.G. (2000). *Walking to the bus rider blues*. New York: Atheneum.
Taylor, M.D. (2001). *Roll of thunder, hear my cry*. New York: Fogelman.
Turner, G.T. (1992). *Take a walk in their shoes*. New York: Puffin.
Curtis, C.P. (1995). *The Watsons go to Birmingham—1963*. New York: Delacorte Press.
Tillage, L. (1997). *Leon's story*. New York: Farrar Straus Giroux.
Taylor, M.D. (1987). *The gold Cadillac*. New York: Dial Books for Young Readers.
Bridges, R. (1999). *Through my eyes*. New York: Scholastic.
Coles, R. (1995). *The story of Ruby Bridges*. New York: Scholastic.

Civics
Mikaelsen, B. (2004). *Touching spirit bear*. Waterville, ME: Thorndike Press.
Avi. (2003). *Nothing but the truth*. New York: Orchard Books.
Bauer, J. (2000). *Hope was here*. New York: Putnam.
Gutman, D. (1996). *The kid who ran for president*. New York: Scholastic.
Gutman, D. (1999). *The kid who became president*. New York: Scholastic.

Death and Illness
Gunther, J.J. (1998). *Death be not proud*. New York: HarperPerennial. (Original work published 1949)
Creech, S. (1994). *Walk two moons*. New York: HarperCollins.
Spinelli, J. (1996). *Crash*. New York: Knopf.
Parks, B. (2000). *The graduation of Jake Moon*. New York: Atheneum.
Bradley, K.B. (2002). *Halfway to the sky*. New York: Delacorte Press.
Bunting, E. (1999). *Blackwater*. New York: Joanna Cotler Books.
Wodson, J. (2003). *Locomotion*. New York: G.P. Putnam's Sons.
D'Amato, B. (2004). *On my honor*. Waterville, ME: Five Star.

Environment
Haissen, C. (2002). *Hoot*. New York: Knopf.
Cleaver, V., & Cleaver, B. (1970). *Where the lilies bloom*. Philadelphia: Lippincott.
George, J.C. (1992). *The missing 'gator of Gumbo Limbo: An ecological mystery*. New York: HarperCollins.
George, J.C. (1998). *My side of the mountain*. New York: Dutton.
George, J.C. (1999). *Frightful's mountain*. New York: Dutton.
George, J.C. (2000). *On the far side of the mountain*. New York: Dutton.

Peer Pressure and Bullying
Bloor, E. (1997). *Tangerine*. San Diego, CA: Harcourt Brace.
Mikaelsen, B. (2004). *Touching spirit bear*. Waterville, ME: Thorndike Press.
Myers, W.D. (1988). *Scorpions*. New York: Harper & Row.
Spinelli, J. (2000). *Stargirl*. New York: Knopf.
Spinelli, J. (1997). *Wringer*. New York: HarperCollins.
Smith, R. (2001). *Zach's lie*. New York: Hyperion.
Spinelli, J. (2002). *Loser*. New York: Joanna Cotler Books.

Note. Titles in each category are arranged from most difficult to least difficult.

Identify materials that will meet the needs of all readers.

Based on my observations of students at the middle level and analysis of informal and standardized reading tests over the past five years, I have found that the reading level of many students varies by approximately two thirds of their age. This means that in a sixth-grade classroom of 12-year-old students, there can be a span of eight years in reading levels. For this reason, there must be not only a variety of genres available at each grade level, but also varying levels of difficulty.

Locate books on a particular topic that are of varying levels. For example, sixth-grade students in Virginia study U.S. history. A teacher with a group of proficient readers may choose to reinforce the social studies curriculum using *The Devil's Arithmetic* (Yolen, 1990). A teacher with an average group of readers may find *Number the Stars* (Lowry, 1989) more appropriate, and a teacher with challenged readers could choose to use *Sadako and the Thousand Paper Cranes* (Coerr, 1977) or *Hiroshima* (Yep, 1995). In order for readers in both groups to show reading growth and become or remain motivated, it is important for them to have materials available at their instructional and independent reading level. (See Table 4.1 for suggested titles listed from the most to the least difficult.)

Provide a variety of reading materials.

The resource collection is far more than a collection of novel sets. Classroom sets of newspapers and periodicals such as *Current Science*, *TIME for Kids*, *READ*, *Kids Discover*, and *Scope* provide teachers with variety, and beginning teachers are often more comfortable working with these resources rather than novels because they are less intimidating. A variety of resources also allows reading specialists the opportunity to provide resources for teachers across the content areas.

Look for user-friendly resource books and novel units.

Novel units are available from a wide variety of companies and their content is often very different. Some novel units offer a series of potential vocabulary words and questions for each chapter, while other units offer enrichment activities and reproducible activities. I did not purchase all of my novel units from one vendor but instead purchased them from several different sources so teachers could have several different formats from which to choose. I have found that the resource books that are checked out most often are the ones that offer graphic organizers and reproducible activities that can be adapted to any story or content area. I also found my personal favorites and received feedback from the teachers about the units that they preferred to use.

When a teacher asks for ideas about how to teach a particular topic, I make sure that I do not simply hand the teacher a book. I use sticky notes to mark pages that have activities, reproducibles, or both that the teacher could use, and then I write a comment on the sticky note about how it can be adapted to meet the teacher's request. I deliver the book personally to the teacher and go over the ideas with him or her. Later, the sticky notes serve as a reminder to the teacher of the ideas we discussed.

Develop a system for requesting, receiving, and replacing materials. Flexibility is the key. If resources are too difficult to obtain, teachers will not use them. Therefore, the door to the resource area should be open at all times, and teachers should be told that they are welcome to come in, have a seat, and browse at any time.

I have found that while I do provide some basic guidelines for checking out resources, each teacher's process for request and check-out is unique. For example, I may receive an e-mail from a teacher requesting 30 copies of *The Giver* (Lowry, 1993) by next Monday, students may pop in with a note from a teacher requesting that I give them 27 copies of *Walk Two Moons* (Creech, 1994), a teacher may come in and request that I help her find a novel that she can use to reinforce her lessons on the U.S. Civil Rights movement, or a teacher may come in while I am gone and check out books on his own.

I provide teachers with a checkout sheet (see Figure 4.4), which I place on a clipboard inside the door, so that they can sign out their materials. It helps me keep track of who has certain materials if another teacher requests them.

When I receive a set of novels or other materials that will be distributed to students, I stamp the top of the book with the school name and number the materials (a great job for a volunteer to do). Through trial and error I learned that the top or bottom of the book is the best place to number them. When I arrived at my school, many of the novel sets had been ordered already so I numbered all the books on the spine with a permanent marker. I was very proud of myself until the first set of books came back from a teacher with half of the numbers rubbed off!

Teachers who allow students to sign out novel sets are provided with a checkout sheet (see Figure 4.5) on which students write their names and the book number that they have been assigned. When the books are collected, the teacher can easily check off whether or not the book has been returned. This sheet is returned to me with the books.

FIGURE 4.4 Reading Resource Materials Checkout Sheet				
Date	Name	Title	# of Books	Date Returned

FIGURE 4.5 Student Novel Checkout Sheet				
Date	Name	Title	Book #	Date Returned

October 22, 2004

Dear Parent or Guardian:
Your child, Erin Smith, was assigned a book from the reading and resource collection. Erin did not return the book and will need to replace it with a new copy or pay for a replacement copy to be purchased. The following book was not returned to Mrs. Lawrence:

Title	Replacement Cost
Lily's Crossing	$4.50

We have worked very hard to build a wonderful collection of class novel sets, and it is important that the books that are lost or damaged be replaced. Please have Erin bring a replacement copy or payment to me by November 5, 2004. Checks should be made payable to Rodney E. Thompson Middle School (Attn: Trade Book Replacement Fund). Thank you for your cooperation.

Sincerely,
Stephanie Pettengill
Reading Specialist

I enter the names of any students who did not return books into a database. Then, I send home a letter to parents of these students and request that either the book be returned or funds are sent to replace the book (see Figure 4.6 for a sample letter). The bookkeeper at my school set up a trade book replacement fund so that any money collected throughout the year could be used to purchase replacement copies.

Concluding Remarks

We have offered many ideas and procedures for setting up a comprehensive literacy program, including building a resource collection consisting of various subjects and difficulty levels. It may seem redundant and obvious, but as we have experienced, these details are critical. Providing time, assistance, and choice for teachers, as well as for students, is critical. The reading specialist, working with the support of other key literacy leaders in the school, can lay the foundation for a successful program with organized and available resources for teachers, parents, and students.

CHAPTER 5

Coordinating and Using Assessment Data

"[I]n reality, assessment is an important part of the total reading program and one that must be planned and implemented as carefully as the curriculum and instructional plans for the school."

Ogle, 2002, p. 137

A FTER YOU HAVE THE necessary resources in place, how do you know which resources are appropriate for each student? Assessment is the answer, but whose responsibility is it? One paradigm for assessment that is sometimes difficult to change is that of the reading specialist doing the reading assessment and the classroom teachers doing the teaching. However, because we believe monitoring progress is central to a successful literacy program in which instruction is differentiated according to student needs (Strickland, Ganske, & Monroe, 2002), monitoring progress through varied assessment needs to be a joint endeavor between the classroom teachers and the reading specialist. If educators perceive assessment as "something the reading specialist does," then assessment results and teaching potential are drastically limited. To make assessments a worthwhile investment in time and energy, assessment needs to be a shared responsibility. Assessment can no longer be the sole responsibility of the reading specialist. When assessment is viewed as an avenue to improve instruction, a variety of assessments can support better teaching, rather than only to remedy students' problem areas (Darling-Hammond, 1994). Thus, by monitoring students' progress, educators can immediately address any tasks that are problematic for students before they become reading difficulties.

A variety of assessments should always be used because each one has a different purpose. The reading specialist can guide teachers to understand which assessments will give teachers the knowledge they need to improve literacy instruction. For example, does the teacher need comprehension information? Is the student having difficulty with content area reading? Is the student's vocabulary knowledge high and comprehension ability low? Reading specialists can ask these types of questions in collaborative meetings with teachers—and often parents, too. The reading specialist can offer recommendations and provide assessments for teachers to use that will provide the information necessary to improve instruction. Most administrators and teachers will be supportive of implementing assessments that help students' literacy development and motivation. And, when teachers feel supported and guided by another expert, such as a reading specialist, they tend to feel validated as a professional and eager to use assessments to improve instruction.

In addition, as discussed in chapter 4, research suggests that time spent reading at a student's independent reading level is imperative to reading growth. Independent reading begins with appropriate reading assessments that help determine what each student's independent reading level is and which resources are necessary.

Share Assessment Responsibilities

When setting up a new school or starting a new reading specialist position, I suggest the reading specialist help teachers check every student's reading level with a "quick and dirty" assessment, such as a short reading inventory. Then, teachers, working within grade-level or team meetings, can check the reading range of the class and inventory the resources in each classroom to see if the books and other materials will meet the students' instructional needs. Administrators usually are responsive to making new purchases when confronted with hard data that shows the educational need for a set of lower or higher level trade books, or to using a different program that is closer to students' instructional needs. Thus, a short reading assessment, combined with careful monitoring of students' classroom work in the first few weeks of the school year, can be used to determine which students need additional diagnostic assessments. Together, teachers and reading specialists can determine which additional assessments can produce the teaching information needed to help each student experience a successful year. Thus, the expert advice of the reading specialist is imperative to students' literacy growth. When the teachers and reading specialists work together and use assessments to inform and guide classroom instruction, students can experience literacy growth and teachers can feel a sense of ownership over classroom instruction and student learning.

Make Assessments Purposeful and Ongoing

Assessments should be ongoing and varied, and used to collect information about each student. However, assessments should never be used in isolation because they do not give a complete picture of a student; they are merely snapshots. A student's interests, prior knowledge, and home situation all contribute to his or her success or lack thereof on any given day with reading or writing assessments. Administrators, parents, students, and policymakers need and deserve assessment information that is systematically collected and analyzed in order to continue to improve instructional support and personal efforts on the part of teachers and students. Just as early literacy assessments can give information critical to students' success, intermediate and upper grade assessments can inform instruction and help determine strategies for students' improvement.

The Reading Specialist Speaks: Using Assessment Results to Improve the Literacy Program

Assessment plays a vital role in the development of a literacy program and must be viewed as a team effort. At my school, a short reading pretest is given to all students at the beginning of the year. This test provides information about students' approximate reading levels and allows us to begin grouping students according to their reading needs and identify students who may be in need of specialized support. Initially, I visited every classroom to administer this test personally. It took students between 30 and 45 minutes to complete the test. Then, I scored the tests electronically and entered the scores into a spreadsheet. It did not take long for me to realize that this was not an effective use of my time, and it caused the testing process to drag out through the entire first month of school. Because the teachers valued the information that this test provided and wanted to have it as soon as possible, it was not difficult for me to enlist their assistance in administering the test. I typed a step-by-step instruction sheet for administering the test (see Table 5.1), provided them with the appropriate materials, and allowed them to administer the test. Thus, an entire team of 100–130 students could complete the test in one class period, rather than 25–30 students as when I was the sole administrator. After students completed the tests, the teachers returned the materials and answer sheets to me. I scored them and entered them into a spreadsheet. With the help of the literacy team, I had a pretest score and approximate reading level documented for every reading student by the middle of the second week of school and was able to focus on assisting with instruction.

Developing and coordinating testing efforts require organization, communication, and flexibility between the reading specialist and the

Administering the Reading Level Indicator

Thank you for administering this reading test to your class. The results will provide us with an estimate of each child's instructional and independent reading level. It will also give us an idea of who may be at risk in the area of literacy so that we can make accommodations that will help students to improve their reading skills. Please follow the guidelines below so that I can get the results of the test compiled and back to you as soon as possible. Please call me if you have any questions.

- Explain to the students that the purpose of this test is to compare the results with their September reading test scores to see how they have improved. This score also will be used to help determine class placement for next year.
- Have students PRINT their first and last name on the blue side of the computer-checked answer sheet. Fill in today's date and on the subject line have them write "reading" and their team name (e.g., Reading–Cool Cat).
- Read the directions for sentence comprehension.
- On the vocabulary section, explain to students that they are looking for the synonym for the underlined word.
- Students are permitted to write on the test if it is a photocopy.
- Students are not to receive any assistance.
- Have the students hold their test materials until everyone has finished. Collect all the tests that have been written on. Collect all the tests that have not been written on. Please give them to me in separate piles so I can destroy the documents that have been written on.
- Return the tests and completed answer sheets to me or drop them in my mailbox.

members of the literacy team. Remember, though, that test administration will vary depending on the test and circumstances at each school. Although classroom teachers may be able to follow instructions and administer a test, such as the reading pretest, specific assessments of individual students and at-risk groups should be done only by a trained special education teacher or reading specialist. In addition, reading specialists should assume full responsibility for interpreting test results. Handing teachers test results without examining the data as a team and explaining what specific terms mean can render the information useless or detrimental (another fact I learned through trial and error).

As I thought about what to include in this chapter I looked carefully at the methods and materials used for assessment at my school. I thought about how I found out about them, how they were administered, what information I gleaned from each of them, and what their advantages and limitations were. Reading specialists can use the following suggestions as they explore different assessment materials and search for what is right for their program.

Examine criteria for state or district assessments.

Find out which grade levels and content areas will be given state or district assessments and when those tests will be administered. Locate resources that are similar in format to the standardized tests so that teachers can familiarize themselves and the students with the format. For example, each year in Virginia the state department releases actual test items from the Standards of Learning tests. These items are valuable resources for teachers and students to use when preparing for the tests.

Confer with the reading supervisor and other reading specialists.

As I have previously mentioned, the networking that occurs between the reading specialists and the reading supervisor offers great direction for all parties involved. In my experience, we have spent countless hours comparing testing materials, discussing advantages and limitations to certain tools, sharing ideas about how to get the literacy team in each building actively involved in the assessment process, and collaboratively interpreting test results to get a clear picture about a student's performance or the effectiveness of a specific reading program. In chapter 3, I mentioned the effectiveness of a common vocabulary among the teachers in my building who had attended the content area reading class. Significant strengths in our school district include the common vocabulary shared by the reading specialists and the consistency in methods and materials that the reading specialists use from school to school.

Identify tests that allow you to examine different aspects of reading.

There are four basic reading assessments that are used throughout my county's reading program: (1) a reading level indicator, which provides an approximate independent and instructional reading level; (2) a reading progress indicator, which can be used to analyze specific areas of weakness in comprehension; (3) a computerized cloze test, which requires students to identify omitted words from sentences or paragraphs; and (4) an individual reading inventory, which requires students to read word lists and passages and orally respond to comprehension passages. Each test has a different format, is administered in a different environment, and provides unique information. See Table 5.2 for a description of each test, its advantages and limitations, and the information it can provide about student performance.

Report on test results promptly.

I have learned that it is critical to analyze and create a report on test scores as soon as testing is completed. I make a valiant attempt to return reading pretest scores to the sixth- and seventh-grade teachers the day after testing has been completed so teachers can use the results to create reading groups based on student needs. In addition, if a teacher or parent has requested that testing be done on a specific student, the flexibility of my schedule allows me to begin testing and provide results in a timely manner to whoever has requested the information.

Present test results in an organized, easy-to-understand format.

When preparing a report, remember that the majority of individuals who will be reading it are not reading specialists. While *instructional reading level, miscue analysis, decoding skills,* and *inference* are words that are second nature to reading specialists and seem to be self-explanatory, it is important to explain these terms so the reader can fully utilize the information being presented. Table 5.3 is an example of a test data spreadsheet that I prepare following the administration of the yearly pretest. I explain the difference between the instructional reading level and independent reading when I meet with individual teachers to create flexible groups and plan instruction (which will be discussed in chapter 6), and I also make written notes on the report to assist teachers if they need to refer to the report at a later date. Table 5.4 is an example of the pre- and posttest report that I prepare at the end of the year. Again, I clarify the terms *instructional reading level* and *independent reading level,* and I use shading to help make the results easier to read. Figure 5.1 illustrates how specific terminology can be clarified in a report so parents or other individuals who may view the report can understand the information. Also, notice that for each type of test I administered (names of specific tests were generalized) I explain what information it is designed to provide, its format, and how it is administered.

Include an easy-to-understand analysis of tests results and practical recommendations.

Figure 5.2 is an example of the analysis of test results and some recommendations that could be made by the reading specialist to help the

TABLE 5.2
Assessment Tools

Assessment	Description	Administration	Advantages	Limitations
Individual Reading Inventory	A series of graded word lists and passages with comprehension questions	Individually, student reads aloud and silently and responds orally	• Checks fluency • Allows for miscue analysis • Keeps students on task	• Takes 30 minutes to 1½ hours per student • Must be administered by reading specialist
Reading Level Indicator	Twenty cloze sentences; twenty items in which students find synonyms	Whole class, untimed	• Short, provides information quickly • Can be administered by classroom teacher • Provides an approximate independent and instructional reading level • Helps identify students in need of assistance or further assessment	• Students with English as a second language tend to score low • Reading specialist must make sure teachers have a clear understanding of reading levels
Reading Progress Indicator	Fiction and nonfiction reading passages with comprehension questions	Whole class, untimed	• Very similar to format of state standardized test • Breaks down question types to easily identify areas of strength and weakness	• Does not provide an approximate grade level • Takes one to two class periods to administer
Computerized Reading Assessment	A series of cloze passages, which get progressively more difficult; student selects one of four answer choices	Individually, timed by computer	• Can be administered to whole class in computer lab setting • Keeps students on task • Detailed report is produced which approximates reading level and suggestions for improving or maintaining skills	• Students sometimes show score higher than on tests that require reading lengthy passages • Very slow readers may miss questions because time runs out

TABLE 5.3
Sample Pretest Score Summary Sheet

Student	Score	InsRdgLvl	IndRdgLvl	Team
Kevin	36		>11.4	Jaguar
Kelly	36		>11.4	Jaguar
Laura	34		11.4	Jaguar
Alexis	33		9.7	Jaguar
Natalie	33		9.7	Jaguar
Andrew	33		9.7	Jaguar
Vince	33		9.7	Jaguar
Greg	32		7.5	Jaguar
Michaela	32		7.5	Jaguar
Brenda	32		7.5	Jaguar
Melissa	32		7.5	Jaguar
Lexi	31		6.5	Jaguar
Sammy	31		6.5	Jaguar
Sarah	31		6.5	Jaguar
Emma	31		6.5	Jaguar
Patrick	30		5.8	Jaguar
Jose	30		5.8	Jaguar
Joseph	30		5.8	Jaguar
Abby	30		5.8	Jaguar
Haleigh	30		5.8	Jaguar
Jeff	30		5.8	Jaguar
Kenny	30		5.8	Jaguar
Jonas	29		5.3	Jaguar
Trey	29		5.3	Jaguar
Gary	29		5.3	Jaguar
Breanna	29		5.3	Jaguar
Chuck	29		5.3	Jaguar
Janey	28		5	Jaguar
George	28		5	Jaguar
Frank	28		5	Jaguar
Martin	28		5	Jaguar
Brooke	28		5	Jaguar
Michaela	27	7.8	4.6	Jaguar
Valerie	27	7.8	4.6	Jaguar
David	27	7.8	4.6	Jaguar
Corey	26	6.8	4.4	Jaguar
Brittany	26	6.8	4.4	Jaguar
Thomas	26	6.8	4.4	Jaguar
Louis	26	6.8	4.4	Jaguar
Caitie	25	6.2	4.2	Jaguar
Lauren	25	6.2	4.2	Jaguar
Erin	24	5.7	4	Jaguar
Bill	24	5.7	4	Jaguar
Heather	23	5.4	3.8	Jaguar
Caleb	21	4.8	3.5	Jaguar
Chrissy	17	3.9	2.9	Jaguar
Allen	12	3.1	2.4	Jaguar

InsRdgLvl = Instructional Reading Level; IndRdgLvl = Independent Reading Level
Note. An average sixth-grade student should have an independent reading level of fifth grade. An instructional level is provided for those students who scored below that point. A standard deviation of approximately one year should be taken into consideration in interpreting these scores.

TABLE 5.4
Sample Pre- and Posttest Report

Name	Sept.	InsRdgLvl	IndRdgLvl	June	InsRdgLvl	IndRdgLvl	Team
Shelly	32		7.5	38		>11.4	Wolves
Allan	35		>11.4	37		>11.4	Wolves
Jacob	32		7.5	37		>11.4	Wolves
Bobby	29		5.3	36		>11.4	Wolves
Tyler	31		6.5	36		>11.4	Wolves
Shanice	32		7.5	35		>11.4	Wolves
Carol	35		>11.4	35		>11.4	Wolves
Cameron	34		11.4	34		11.4	Wolves
Martin	35		>11.4	34		11.4	Wolves
Kristie	32		7.5	34		11.4	Wolves
Thomas	33		9.7	33		9.6	Wolves
Cole	30		5.8	33		9.6	Wolves
Molly	30		5.8	32		7.4	Wolves
Bethany	31		6.5	32		7.4	Wolves
Jonathan	28	9.5	5	31		6.5	Wolves
Abigail	30		5.8	31		6.5	Wolves
George	29		5.3	30		5.8	Wolves
Matthew	29		5.3	30		5.8	Wolves
Erin	27	7.8	4.6	30		5.8	Wolves
Colin	23	5.4	3.8	30		5.8	Wolves
Aubrey	22	5.1	3.6	29		5.3	Wolves
Jake	26	6.8	4.4	29		5.3	Wolves
Chrissy	24	5.7	4	29		5.3	Wolves
Jacqueline	28	9.5	5	29		5.3	Wolves
Ella	29		5.3	28	9.5	5	Wolves
Samantha	24	5.7	4	28	9.5	5	Wolves
Nicole	27	7.8	4.6	27	7.8	4.6	Wolves
Heather	25	6.3	4.2	27	7.8	4.6	Wolves
Andrew	27	7.8	4.6	27	7.8	4.6	Wolves
Devin	26	6.8	4.4	27	7.8	4.6	Wolves
Allie	23	5.4	3.8	27	7.8	4.6	Wolves
Heather	20	4.5	3.3	26	6.8	4.4	Wolves
Clifford	31		6.5	26	6.8	4.4	Wolves
Donald	23	5.4	3.8	26	6.8	4.4	Wolves
Katherine	22	5.1	3.6	25	6.3	4.2	Wolves
Trent	19	4.3	3.2	22	5.1	3.6	Wolves
Daphne	23	5.4	3.8	21	4.8	3.5	Wolves
Mark	19	4.3	3.2	21	4.8	3.5	Wolves

InsRdgLvl = Instructional Reading Level; IndRdgLvl = Independent Reading Level
Note. September and June scores reflect number correct out of 40 items.

indicates a higher posttest score.

indicates a posttest score the same as the pretest score.

indicates a lower posttest score.

FIGURE 5.1
Sample Reading Report

Student: David   **Evaluator: Stephanie Pettengill**
Grade: 8   **Reading Specialist**

Reading/Classroom Attitude

David was very cooperative during the testing. He was initially concerned that he was in trouble for something, but relaxed when I explained what the purpose of our meeting was. David said that he likes to read and especially likes to read sports magazines. He spoke frequently about his favorite sports during the testing period. He said that most reading was easy for him, but that Social Studies was hard because of the names of people and places. We discussed the novel he was currently reading in class, The Orphan of Ellis Island, and he appeared enthusiastic about the story. He was able to tell me what had happened in the story, but the events were not in sequence.

Individual Reading Inventory

An Individual Reading Inventory was administered to David. He was asked to read word lists and short passages aloud and answer comprehension questions. David and I were the only ones in the room and there were no outside distractions.

Sight Words/Decoding

Decoding is the ability to figure out unfamiliar words by using letter sounds or breaking the words into recognizable parts. David had very little difficulty with the words on the third through sixth grade lists. He missed an average of three words on each list, but could usually decode them when asked to read them again. On the seventh grade list he was able to recognize 9/20 immediately and use decoding skills to identify one more. His errors are logical and show that he is using decoding skills effectively.

Reading Passages/Comprehension

Comprehension is the ability to understand and recall the information that has been read. David read a fifth and sixth grade passage with very little difficulty. He read fairly fluently and did not appear to have any tracking difficulties. He was able to answer 9.5/10 questions correctly on the fifth grade passage. He answered 6/10 correctly on the sixth grade passage. According to the results of the Individual Reading Inventory, David is reading at an instructional level of sixth grade. *The instructional reading level is the level at which a student can read and comprehend with guidance from the teacher concerning new vocabulary and ideas. A sixth grade student should be at an instructional reading level of sixth grade, which indicates that David is reading on grade level.* The specific results of his testing are attached.

Computer Diagnostic Report

The Computer Diagnostic is taken to identify the approximate reading level of a student and to provide information about his performance compared to other students at the same grade level. The computer program presents the students with a series of 25 cloze passages. *In a cloze passage, a word is left out of a sentence or paragraph. The student must read the passage and select the answer choice that makes sense.* The passages become progressively more difficult as the test continues. According to the results of the Computer Diagnostic, David is reading at an instructional level (grade equivalency) of 4.2. His independent reading level is approximately 3.9. The results of the Computer Diagnostic are attached.

Vocabulary Test

The Vocabulary Test is a 40 question test designed to provide an estimate of a student's instructional and independent reading level. The first twenty items are statements in which a word is left out. The student is asked to select the word in a group of 4–5 that makes the most sense. The remainder of the test is statements in which the student must select the *synonym, or word that means the same as,* a highlighted word in the statement. In September, David scored 16/40. This test was administered in a classroom setting. The Vocabulary Test results indicate that David is reading at an instructional level of 3.8 and an independent level of 2.8.

Analysis of Test Results

The Vocabulary Test and the Individual Reading Inventory have been administered to numerous students in the building from September 2001 to the present. I have found that the results of the tests are usually very consistent with each other. David, however, showed a discrepancy of over two years difference between the instructional reading level indicated by the Vocabulary Test and the instructional reading level indicated by the IRI. David's inconsistent scores indicate that environmental factors play a large role in his academic performance. During the IRI, David remained on task because he was reading to me and answering questions that I asked him orally. During the vocabulary test and the Computer Diagnostic he was required to keep himself on-task, which proved to be more difficult. David's academic difficulties do not appear to be the result of a specific decoding or comprehension problem, but rather a result of difficulty attending to classroom tasks and remaining focused on the text or assignments.

Considering all factors, David's instructional reading level is estimated at about fifth grade. An average sixth grade student reads at an instructional sixth grade level. In a small group setting David could be expected to perform at a higher level. In a large group, his ability to comprehend material will be hindered.

Recommendations

David would be most successful in a setting which would allow small group work, monitoring of skills, and minimal distractions. Instruction in various study strategies, note-taking, and organizational skills would be helpful for David. He would benefit from the support of a mentor, counselor, or teacher (other than his team teachers) who could monitor his progress. David should be encouraged to read independently each day in order to maintain and strengthen his reading skills. He should read a variety of materials such as novels, newspapers, and magazines so that he can become familiar with different types of print formats.

---

student succeed. This example illustrates how valuable a variety of assessment types is in getting a clear picture of a student's reading ability. Had I stopped with the Individual Reading Inventory or depended on the vocabulary test as my only source of information, my report would have been very different and would not have been beneficial to anyone. In addition to the analysis, every test report should include practical, easy-to-implement suggestions for the classroom teacher and for the parents to follow. It is not enough to identify a student's current ability; reading specialists must also provide suggestions on how to help the student succeed in the future.

Concluding Remarks

Teaching and assessment should be constant, ongoing occurrences in most classrooms. Ongoing assessments help provide students with feelings of self-efficacy because they are able to realize when they are reading material at their appropriate instructional level. The challenge is to use a variety of assessments and then use the results appropriately and efficiently, so all students can experience success and see growth in their reading and writing abilities. We recommend that students, when at all possible, be involved and participate in ongoing growth plans so that each student assumes ownership over his or her reading progress. When all students strive to better themselves as readers and writers, reading becomes an acceptable practice and does not carry a negative stigma.

CHAPTER 6

Planning and Collaborating With Teachers

*"[S]chools must provide classroom
teachers with reading specialist
services, including resource support,
current research on reading and
learning, and ongoing staff
development through self study...."*

Vacca, 2002, p. 187

THE NEXT PART OF the literacy program model focuses on leadership in instruction, which includes planning and collaborating with classroom teachers. Planning appropriate instruction can be a formidable task for any teacher, whether he or she is responsible for 24 elementary students, 120 middle or high school level students, or 8 special needs students. It is quite common for a teacher to have students with reading abilities that range from four to eight grade levels, as well as fluctuating maturity and interest levels. Therefore, most teachers welcome assistance as they plan appropriate instruction for their students, and the reading specialist's expertise and experience is a tremendous help. Most teachers understand the importance of having each student connect with literacy— with a book, magazine, or literacy-related task the student wants to accomplish—so it is essential to have materials and flexible groups to facilitate this connection with every student. The reading specialist's expert knowledge of the available literature and students' needs and interests can be an invaluable resource to teachers as they attempt to reach all of their students.

Ogle (2002) suggests some essential conditions that promote effective collaborations between reading specialists and classroom teachers. First, time for planning, sharing, and adapting with the reading specialist and teachers is essential. Second, an open school culture is essential for teamwork and sharing. When reading specialists and teachers work together in a nonjudgmental atmosphere, the environment is much more conducive to working and learning and, thus, benefits students and teachers. Finally, teachers and students must have a shared vision of literacy and a shared commitment toward a similar goal—for example, teachers and students might make a commitment to a reading incentive such as we did with the Virginia Young Readers Program because of their shared vision of literacy.

Teachers usually are most comfortable teaching the way they learn best, whether it be through individual response or in group discussions. Ogle (2002) suggests that reading specialists work collaboratively with teachers to expand their teaching repertoire to include a variety of strategies and responses. Therefore, reading specialists should be well versed in a variety of ways to make literacy learning enjoyable as well profitable for most students. In their work as reading coaches to teachers in the classroom setting, reading specialists may be able to suggest methods teachers may have overlooked or have not been exposed to in previous teaching experiences.

Preparing Strategies to Share

Every school year the reading specialists in our district meet monthly to discuss district business, reading research, and reading strategies. As the supervisor, I serve as the facilitator of each meeting. Each year, the reading specialists choose several reading strategies to model, based on their review of assessment scores for their schools and for the district and on the basis of the reading specialists' informal classroom observations. The state assessment scores help inform instruction in specific areas, such as comprehension and word analysis. For example, one year after careful review of assessment results and discussion, as a group we focused on becoming experts in lessons on Question–Answer Relationships (Raphael, 1986) and modeling these lessons for teachers. This strategy aids in comprehension by teaching students that there are usually four types of comprehension questions generated after reading a text. When students know the different types of questions, they can learn how to answer the questions in the best way possible. Another year, the reading specialists chose to focus on parts of the writing process because they were disappointed with the district writing scores. Each specialist developed lessons according to his or her school's needs in order to provide focused writing instruction to help with student performance on the writing test. Last year, the reading specialists determined that we needed to build family support and practice at home, so we concentrated on parent involvement activities. When we met once a month, we shared and discussed activities to involve the parents, such as reading nights, writing nights, book fairs, open library nights, cooking centers, spooky story night, storytelling and Readers Theatre, and coffee house poetry night. We discussed all planning and implementation details so other reading specialists could gain ideas from other schools' successful literacy events. For example, one reading specialist shared the details of "Milk and Cookies Night," an event held at a middle school. Teachers, students, and their parents were encouraged to come back to school for a "bedtime snack" of milk and cookies (provided by the Parent–Teacher Organization) while teachers read aloud in their classroom from their favorite "bedtime reading," with light classical music playing in the background. Students also were encouraged to bring their favorite books to read aloud or silently. All teachers who participated remarked on the ease of implementation and how much everyone enjoyed the evening, and teachers and parents suggested repeating it during the next semester.

With the pressure of high-stakes testing and curriculum requirements, there often is not enough time during the school day for modeling and sharing the joy of reading; however, the reality is that students will not improve without consistent time to practice reading. By sharing their lessons and team teaching experiences, the reading specialists helped one another develop a wealth of teaching tools.

Collaborative Planning Includes Administrators

As the literacy team works to help parents become partners in literacy development by showing them different ways in which they can be involved, they also work with administrators so they can support literacy development throughout the school year. Involving the administration is critical to a successful literacy program because administrators can support the program by prioritizing time for literacy events and valuing and ensuring reading and writing time. Administrators' decisions affect every aspect of the school's total literacy program, from scheduling to funding, from time out of the classroom to observe and plan with peers and support for collaborative teaching arrangements to purchasing appropriate materials (Moore, 2000). Administrators are responsible for a myriad of daily tasks, so it is not practical to expect them to be knowledgeable regarding the latest research and suggestions regarding literacy instruction. Reading specialists in our district help administrators by sharing with them important articles from professional journals, relevant teaching ideas, and materials.

As a district-level supervisor, I welcome the opportunity several times a year to present research to the administrators and to discuss literacy-related teaching suggestions with administrators in the elementary, middle, or high school principal meeting setting. I often begin with a K-W-L (Ogle, 1986), where I ask principals to focus on what they Know about a topic, such as fluency; what they Want to learn about it; and what they have Learned after a discussion. Writing this information on a three-column graphic organizer helps the group keep track of the discussion. I end the session with a "ticket out" technique, where principals are required to write a question, statement, or individual concern and give it to me when leaving. I have found this activity to be non-threatening and beneficial because administrators welcome the "nuggets" of information and feel valued as learners, while not feeling threatened as instructional leaders. I address these questions individually or, if appropriate, I use the question as a topic of discussion during the next meeting.

As instructional leaders, principals are often responsible for evaluating teachers in many disciplines and appreciate guidelines or specific things they can look for in different areas of instruction. I provide an observation guide for principals to use in making their observations and a note sheet on which they can make notes for follow-up meetings with the teacher. (See Figure 6.1A for the observation guide and Figure 6.1B for the accompanying note sheet.) Reading specialists also can share these guidelines with teachers, so teachers can use them to help plan their instruction.

According to Vacca (2002), "schools must provide classroom teachers with reading specialist services, including resource support, current research on reading and learning, and ongoing staff development" (p. 187). Team planning and teaching opportunities are also beneficial services that may help result in positive feelings of self-efficacy for the classroom teacher and students.

The Reading Specialist Speaks: Planning and Collaborating With Teachers

A strong literacy program requires collaboration, and collaboration requires time to share thoughts and ideas. Examples of planning and collaboration appear in every chapter of this book because they are the cornerstones of a strong reading program. The things that you do to set up the literacy program, to build your literacy community, to develop a resource collection, and to assess students all require planning and collaboration. Planning and collaboration occur not only with the teachers in your specific building

FIGURE 6.1A
Observation Guide for Supervisors and Administrators

Reading

In this classroom, is the teacher
- modeling and sharing his or her own joy of reading?
- recommending books of interest to students?
- providing a variety of literature genres (e.g., short stories, novels, poetry, biographies, essays, informational books, magazines)?
- providing time for daily, self-selected silent reading?
- reading aloud to students on a daily basis?
- requiring a minimum of oral reading practice by the students (and providing silent practice before any oral reading)?
- incorporating thematic units in language arts instruction?
- providing skills (e.g., phonics) instruction for those needing it, not in isolation but within meaningful contexts?
- utilizing a variety of grouping strategies for instruction (e.g., whole class, flexible small groups, partners, cooperative learning groups)?
- providing opportunities for students to read independently and work individually on some tasks?
- utilizing strategies that promote discussion, divergent thinking, and multiple responses?
- assigning reading tasks that promote collaboration and cooperation among students?
- planning reading tasks and strategies that activate and utilize students' prior knowledge before, during, and after reading?
- asking questions that encourage and promote dialogue, inquiry, and critique?
- encouraging a variety of responses to literature and to questions that are asked about the literature?
- collecting portfolio assessment data that is authentic in nature (e.g., transcribed, taped, or analyzed retelling) and selected for inclusion by the student and teacher so that the student, parents, and teacher are all involved in assessing progress?
- using portfolio data to guide instructional decisions and individual instruction?

Writing

In this classroom, is the teacher
- modeling and sharing his or her joy of writing?
- modeling and teaching the stages of the writing process (prewriting, drafting, sharing, revising, editing, publishing)?
- assigning daily writing for a variety of purposes to a variety of audiences?
- encouraging divergent, creative thinking through writing assignments?
- encouraging students to use their writing as a natural response to literature?
- incorporating invented ("temporary") spelling strategies for beginning readers and writers?
- encouraging more mature writers to attempt invented spellings when composing, then assisting them with checking for correct spellings during editing?
- regularly conferring with each student about his or her writing?
- responding to student writing with helpful suggestions, thoughtful comments, and very little "red-marking"?
- promoting student self-assessment and peer conferences for the revision and editing stages?

(continued)

- displaying and publishing student writing?
- collecting portfolio assessment data that is authentic in nature (e.g., samples of writing in various stages and journal entries) and selected for inclusion by the student and teacher so that the student, parents, and teacher all are involved in assessing progress?
- using portfolio data to guide instructional decisions and individual instruction?

Listening
In this classroom, is the teacher
- promoting listening as a means of learning?
- providing opportunities for students to hear other students' responses to the literature they have read?
- providing a variety of listening experiences for differing purposes (e.g., "sharing" time, reports, Readers Theatre, students' rehearsed oral reading)?
- reading aloud to students from narrative and expository texts and from poetry selections?
- providing discussion opportunities for students to collaborate, cooperate, and compromise?
- promoting social skills through listening (e.g., providing and maintaining eye contact, paraphrasing to demonstrate understanding, and summarizing what was heard)?

Speaking
In this classroom, is the teacher
- providing daily opportunities for structured oral language development (e.g., choral reading, speeches, dramas, "sharing" time, oral reports, debates, discussion)?
- modeling and teaching correct language usage?
- teaching students to facilitate group discussion?
- modeling and teaching language for a variety of purposes (e.g., informing, persuading, sharing feelings, evaluating, imagining, predicting)?
- using literature and student writing as a source for oral language development?

General
In this classroom, is the teacher
- actively observing and noting or recording students' responses and participation during reading/language arts instruction?
- enabling all children to make choices about what they read and write?
- resisting labeling students in terms of ability or achievement?
- communicating to parents the tenets of integrated reading/language arts instruction?
- encouraging parents to read to their children, discuss literature with them, and support and encourage their children's reading and writing progress?
- providing a structured reading environment where opinion, creative thought, and sharing of ideas are valued?
- celebrating literacy and learning on a daily basis?
- participating in staff development and then attempting to implement newly learned ideas?

From Vogt, M.E. (1991). An observation guide for supervisors and administrators: Moving toward integrated reading/language arts instruction. *The Reading Teacher, 45*(3), 206–211.

FIGURE 6.1B
Administrator's Note Sheet for Teacher Observation

Teacher_____ Date_____

Teaching English/reading

Evidence of
_____
Building and/or connecting prior knowledge

_____
Teaching and/or reviewing vocabulary

_____
Motivating and/or setting purpose for students

_____
Engaging students in a personal response to text

_____
Helping students with text structures

_____
Creating and supporting a caring environment
  • Teaching students to monitor and repair

  • Scaffolding support for students

_____
Making reading and writing connections

_____
Additional Observations

_____

but also with educators and reading specialists from other schools in your district. When I came on board as a new middle school specialist, I depended tremendously on the knowledge and experiences of my colleagues. Now it is my pleasure to be in the position to share this knowledge with you. The following specific suggestions will help reading specialists make collaboration a part of the reading program.

Develop clear guidelines for reading teachers to follow.

The reading programs at each of the middle schools in the county where I work are unique; however, the responsibilities of the reading teacher seemed to be a common area of concern among some teachers and administrators. They raised questions as to whether the reading teacher or the language arts teacher was responsible for covering the state reading objectives. The goal of the districtwide literacy committee in creating a separate reading program was that the students would receive reading instruction from the language arts teacher using the grade-level literature book and the reading teacher would reinforce those concepts and strengthen students' comprehension and vocabulary using novels at their instructional and independent level. The committee, including me, realized that in order to accomplish our goal, we had to make the objectives of the reading program clear. A team of reading teachers, the middle school reading specialists, and the reading supervisor met over the summer to develop a reading curriculum. We decided that the reading class would be entitled Reading Enrichment in order to clarify that it was *in addition* to the reading instruction provided by the language arts teacher. We developed a course description and curriculum objectives and combined them into a course card for each grade level (see Figure 6.2). We then compiled a reading enrichment curriculum binder. The binder included an easy-to-understand description of the reading process, active reading strategies, a curriculum checklist (see Figures 6.3 and 6.4), lesson plan ideas, graphic organizers, the county language arts curriculum, the county list of approved trade books, and the trade book rationale form.

Present and discuss the guidelines you have created.

Because the committee had worked so hard on the reading curriculum and because it was so user friendly, we wanted to make sure teachers knew what was in the prepared binder. Handing busy teachers the binder or putting it in their mailboxes would not have ensured that they would get the full benefit of the valuable information included. We decided

Sixth-Grade Reading Enrichment Course Card
Reading Enrichment Course Description:
Reading is essential to learning in all subject areas. Reading is a process that includes three phases: before reading, during reading, and after reading. Teachers will provide instruction in and modeling of effective reading strategies that will help students become active, purposeful, and increasingly independent learners through the use of authentic literature. The reading program will focus on vocabulary knowledge, in addition to teaching critical reading and comprehension skills.

Sixth-Grade Reading Enrichment Curriculum
Course Objectives:
• Make predictions from prior knowledge and text
• Identify the source, viewpoint, and purpose of text
• Identify information, such as facts and details from narrative and expository text
• Learn to self-monitor for comprehension
• Summarize important information from text
• Apply appropriate self-questioning strategies
• Compare and contrast author's style
• Develop vocabulary and word meanings through the use of context clues, root words, and affixes
• Understand word choice and how words and structure convey author's point of view (example: jargon, figurative language, dialect)
• Use writing-to-learn techniques including learning logs, journals, notes, and outlines
• Learn effective use of study guides
• Use word reference materials
• Expand knowledge of word origins
• Identify the best source to find information
• Use graphic organizers to organize and remember information
• Improve reading fluency

Developed by the Reading Enrichment Curriculum Committee for Stafford County Public Schools.

that we would meet with our reading teachers and go through the binder together creating and inserting tabs for each section, thus allowing teachers to become familiar with the material. We prepared the binders with all the necessary pages, provided teachers with tab dividers for each section, and then walked them through the curriculum—allowing time for questions and discussion. The language arts teachers received this information during the countywide meeting during the teacher workweek in August. In my building, all sixth- and seventh-grade teachers teach reading, so I asked to meet with them during their monthly grade-level meeting. Although this meeting was held a few weeks after school began, I felt

FIGURE 6.3
Sample Curriculum Checklist

Comprehension															
Set Purpose for Reading															
Activate Prior Knowledge															
Expand Prior Knowledge															
Predict															
Formulate Questions															
Clarify/Self-Monitor															
Visualize															
Summarize															
Sequence Events															
Identify Main Idea															
Determine Fact and Opinion															
Recognize Cause and Effect															
Compare and Contrast															
Make Inferences															
Written Responses															
Vocabulary															
Vocabulary Building															
Word Origins															
Roots/Suffixes/Prefixes															
Figurative Language															
Context Clues															
Oral Language															
Reading Aloud															
Partner Reading															
Choral Reading															
Readers Theatre															
Oral Presentations															
Fluency															
Study Skills															
Note-Taking															
Two-Column Notes															
Outline/Power Notes															
SQ3R															
Graphic Organizers															
Story Map															
Event Map															
K-W-L															
Venn Diagram															
Genre															
Fiction															
Science Fiction															
Fantasy															
Mystery															
Realistic Fiction															
Historical Fiction															
Nonfiction															
Biography															
Autobiography															
Current Events															
Informational Text															
Newspaper/Magazines															
Poetry															
Plays															
Other:															

FIGURE 6.4
Sample Curriculum Checklist in Use

	Tuck Everlasting/Babbitt	Children of the Dust Bowl/Stanley	Out of the Dust/Hesse	The Westing Game/Raskin
Comprehension				
Set Purpose for Reading	✓	✓	✓	✓
Activate Prior Knowledge	✓	✓	✓	
Expand Prior Knowledge		✓	✓	
Predict	✓		✓	✓
Formulate Questions	✓			✓
Clarify/Self-Monitor				✓
Visualize	✓			✓
Summarize	✓	✓	✓	
Sequence Events	✓		✓	✓
Identify Main Idea			✓	
Determine Fact and Opinion		✓		✓
Recognize Cause and Effect	✓	✓	✓	✓
Compare and Contrast	✓	✓	✓	✓
Make Inferences	✓			✓
Written Responses			✓	✓
Vocabulary				
Vocabulary Building	✓	✓		
Word Origins	✓			
Roots/Suffixes/Prefixes	✓			
Figurative Language	✓		✓	✓
Context Clues	✓	✓		✓
Oral Language				
Reading Aloud			✓	✓
Partner Reading	✓			✓
Choral Reading			✓	
Readers Theatre				
Oral Presentations		✓		✓
Fluency			✓	
Study Skills				
Note-Taking		✓		
Two-Column Notes				
Outline/Power Notes				
SQ3R		✓		
Graphic Organizers				
Story Map				
Event Map			✓	
K-W-L		✓		
Venn Diagram	✓			
Genre				
Fiction				
Science Fiction				
Fantasy	✓			
Mystery				✓
Realistic Fiction				
Historical Fiction			✓	
Nonfiction				
Biography				
Autobiography				
Current Events				
Informational Text		✓		
Newspaper/Magazines				
Poetry			✓	
Plays				
Other:				
Compare with movie	✓			
Free-form/Picture map		✓		
Create graphic org. to keep track of charac.				✓

84

that teachers understood and appreciated the information much more at that point. As most educators know, the beginning of the school year is an endless succession of meetings, information packets, attendance sheets, and procedure reviews. If I had held the meeting earlier, the binder likely would have become just one more thing in the pile.

Meet with teams or grade levels to discuss assessment results and create flexible groups.

Once the pretest discussed in chapter 5 is completed, I meet with the team teachers to examine the results. I make enough copies of the results (see Table 5.3, page 67) for each member of the team and explain the report. We examine the data, consider any additional information that we have about the students (e.g., performance from the previous year, state assessment scores, motivation and attitude), and divide the class into two, three, or four reading groups depending on the number of teachers on the team. The groups with the highest readers are large, and the group with the lower readers are kept as small as possible. For example, on a four-person team with 107 students the highest reading group may have 35 students, the high–average group may have 30, the low–average group 24, and the lowest group 18. The important thing to remember about these groups is that they are flexible. If a student is placed in the lowest reading group and shows improvement, he or she can be moved to a higher group. If a student is in a higher group and seems to need more direct instruction or is not performing well, he or she can be moved to a more appropriate group.

Design a reading model that works best for each team.

Over the past four years, a wide variation of reading configurations has been tried at Thompson Middle School. As I previously mentioned, my role throughout this time has been to offer guidance, document what has and has not been successful, and to facilitate change when necessary. I remain open minded and welcome suggestions and change, but I am also careful to maintain aspects that have proven to be successful, such as providing time for reading, using flexible grouping, selecting appropriate materials, and motivating teachers. How do you motivate teachers? In addition to the suggestions in chapters 2 and 3, teacher motivation also occurs when teachers are allowed to make decisions about the reading model for their team. Some teams prefer to keep the same group of students all year long, while some like to switch groups at the semester break, and others like to rotate the students every six weeks so each teacher has the opportunity to teach the students across the reading ability spectrum. Some teams prefer that I pull out small groups of students for instruction, and others prefer that I come into the classroom. Based on data that I have examined in past years, there is no one model that proves to be the most successful for student achievement. What matters is the motivation of the teachers. As we examined test data, created groups, and made decisions about the reading classes together, teachers began to take ownership of the reading program. They were eager to examine the pretest scores and discuss the best way to group the students, and they were even more eager to see the results of the posttest after a year of hard work. They made the decisions about whether to keep the same group of students all year or rotate them each grading period and which materials they would use. Again, there is not one best model, but by making sure essential elements, such as those previously listed, are in place and listening to the needs of the literacy team, the reading specialist can help teachers develop a system that works for them and their students.

Be available for collaboration and planning by maintaining a flexible schedule.

As mentioned throughout this book, it is important for reading specialists to maintain a flexible schedule. In order to make sure there is time for collaboration and planning, you need to be familiar with the master schedule—what period each team has reading and when each grade level has their planning time. For example, as I mentioned earlier, I know that the sixth-grade teachers in my building have their planning time during second and third period. If I were assigned a class during those periods all year, I would not be available for collaboration and planning with the sixth-grade teachers until after school. When I am planning classroom instruction, small-group sessions, or both, I keep some time available when I know each grade level has planning so that they have the opportunity to come in at their convenience. In addition, the reading/resource room should have an open-door policy, and when a teacher enters the room, his or her needs should take priority. It is also important to keep in mind certain times of the school year when teachers may need to plan and choose resources. For example, I know that the week before the grading period ends, most seventh-grade teachers come to me looking for new novels for their reading classes and for resources to go with it. I make sure that during that week, fourth and fifth periods are free so that I can meet with these teachers and help them plan their next novel unit. One teacher selected the Dive trilogy by Gordon Korman to use with her students and wanted to get some ideas about how to introduce the specific vocabulary associated with scuba diving and underwater exploration to her class and how to get students motivated. Rather than just suggesting a few ideas, we sat down together, came up with a plan, and taught the unit together. The students spent the first week doing research in the library. They prepared a group presentation, presented it to the class, and when we began to read the book, they were excited. They did not stumble over terms such as *buoyancy compensator*, *regulator*, or *compressed air* because they were familiar with them. They were able to comprehend what was happening in the story and create a visual picture because they had built each other's background knowledge through their presentations. Had I simply offered a few suggestions, handed the teacher a resource book, or offered to pull out a small group of students, the results would not have been nearly as good. By collaborating and planning with teachers, reading specialists can create a situation in which everyone wins: The teacher learned from me, I learned from her, and all of the students in the class benefited from our combined efforts.

Concluding Remarks

The reading specialist's role as a collaborative leader requires empathy, understanding, and resilience. The reading specialist must be a hard-working member of the faculty and an equal to teachers yet also be able to advise and assist teachers at each grade level. We strive to have the reading specialist be a member of the school community by participating in school-related duties and after-school responsibilities. However, keeping the duties manageable, such as a highly visible front door duty or an open computer lab monitor, allows the reading specialist to share equally as one of the staff while maintaining a visible and accessible presence every day in school life. Thus, planning questions, resource questions, and assessment questions all can be handled with immediacy, and the literacy program as a whole can be seen as a natural part of everyone's school day. Successful collaborative efforts ultimately result in teachers who are more actively involved in classroom and schoolwide literacy efforts and who feel better prepared to more effectively meet their students' needs.

CHAPTER 7

Supporting Classroom Instruction

"[S]pecialists have the knowledge base to provide classroom teachers with the support they need to learn new content and research based instruction and to assist teachers as they practice new strategies and programs in their classrooms."

Dole, 2004, p. 465

NOTHER ELEMENT OF INSTRUCTION in the literacy program model is supporting classroom instruction, which includes organization. Having the knowledge to coordinate a schoolwide literacy program is only the first step in developing a successful reading program. It also requires a great deal of preparation and flexibility. As a supervisor, I resist the pressure to mandate requirements; rather, I have learned to use each reading specialist to facilitate work with the administration and the literacy committee, and to collaboratively determine the course for each school. We set guidelines; for example, each school must have time built into the program for independent reading in addition to the language arts block, and each school must actively involve parents. Each school is also required to implement thoughtful reading incentive programs (see chapter 9 for more information about these programs) and to conduct meaningful staff development sessions according to the needs of each staff (see Figure 3.2, page 39, for a sample listing of mini-inservice lessons). The staff development plan must be developed according to the individual educational needs of each staff and student community. The staffs' needs will determine the extent of time that the specialist devotes to each instructional area. Currently, staff members at several schools are well trained in content reading strategies, after several years of modeling and school-based staff development. The reading specialists at those schools are working on process writing strategies and study skills in particular this year. Teachers and administrators at other schools have now expressed interest in having more training in content reading strategies, while other buildings wish to work on independent and guided reading strategies in order to build the reading stamina of its students. The focus must come from the key players, the school literacy committee, and be based in part on test scores and observed student and teacher needs. Only by having school-based goals will the instruction in each classroom truly support the goal.

It has been our experience that teachers welcome another person delivering similar reading messages when working toward a shared instructional goal. It is the responsibility of the reading specialist to connect with every teacher, sometime in the first six weeks of the school year, to find out in what areas the teacher would appreciate some reinforcement assistance. At the start of every year, the reading specialist must establish himself or herself as a member of each instructional team or grade level, and make informal, anecdotal notes, which can later be used to determine programs and materials. As the reading specialist walks the halls, he or she may be asked to check on a student or locate some materials on a specific subject. When a reading specialist can respond to teachers' inquiries in a timely manner, it enhances the credibility of the reading specialist as a team player.

At each school in our district we begin every school year by emphasizing at faculty meetings and at parent meetings that reading well means comprehending well. Too often, we hear from parents, and even from teachers, comments such as, "My student is a good reader; he or she just cannot comprehend." We make it clear, however, that reading is not simply decoding; reading is gaining meaning from print. By conveying this message, we hope parents gain a better understanding of the reading program so we can enlist their support. Our focus as a school district is active reading for active thinking. This is the time for high levels of literacy achievement expected for all students. "To achieve the universally high standards of literacy now called for, schools must reconceptualize literacy teaching and learning and craft school programs that provide a more coherent and comprehensive instructional plan" (Allington, 2002, p. 282). Through a program model that focuses on shared responsibility and planning and facilitating instruction in a team approach, reading specialists can support classroom instruction and help more students meet current literacy demands.

The Reading Specialist Speaks: Planning and Organizing

In order for a reading specialist to effectively provide classroom instruction, an organizational system must be in place for scheduling and keeping track of materials. Organization has always been a challenge for me, and when I began the job as literacy leader I realized that I was going to have to make it priority. Having a flexible schedule has been the best way for me to meet the needs of the student and teacher populations in my building, but it does present challenges. You become responsible for making sure that your time is used effectively without overscheduling to the point where you are no longer an available resource. I also found that a conventional planner or lesson plan book really did not work well for me because my schedule varied from day to day, so I created my own. Reading specialists can use the information and ideas in the following section to help organize their days and schedule classroom instruction to better meet students' and teachers' needs.

Create a planning binder.

■ Purchase a one-inch ring binder with a window front and inside pockets. Choose a color that you do not typically use so that you can easily locate the folder. For example, I keep all of my presentations in white binders, but my planner is bright blue so I can locate it quickly without having to search for it.

■ Consider what information needs to be easily accessible on a daily or weekly basis and set up sections using tab dividers. For example, as a building resource, you will constantly refer to the master schedule. Include the master schedule and a listing of staff members' names and room numbers in one section.

■ Dedicate a section to resource requests and scheduling. Figures 7.1 and 7.2 are sources that I use to create my schedule and keep track of resource requests. On Monday morning, make a copy of Figure 7.2 and post it on your door so that staff members know where you are and when you will be available. Copy the weekly planner on the back of the weekly schedule (Figure 7.3) so you can open your binder and see your week without flipping back and forth. Figures 7.4 and 7.5 show what a completed week might look like. Note that items in the priorities section of Figure 7.4 are listed in order of importance.

■ Designate a section for essential information such as course descriptions, course cards, and curriculum and state standards for reading. You also can insert trade book lists and resource lists.

■ Include a section with student test data. This can be helpful for identifying students for reading groups and for planning instruction. As discussed in chapter 5, each year the students in all grade levels are given a reading pretest. I enter those scores on a spreadsheet and give copies to each teacher on the team. I also place a copy in my binder

World War II Book Talk

I am available this week during the following times.
Sign your name (and room number) by your preferred class period.

Tuesday, September 14   Wednesday, September 15

Period 1   Period 1

Period 2   Period 2

Period 3

Period 5   Period 5

Period 6   Period 6

You will receive confirmation in one to two days. Thank You.
I look forward to working with you and your class.

in the student data section. This information serves as a quick reference as to which team a student is on and his or her approximate reading level. I use this information constantly when scheduling small groups, classroom instruction, and individual testing. It also allows me to recognize which teams have large groups of at-risk students and may need extra assistance.

FIGURE 7.2
Weekly Planner

Week of _____

Priorities:
1. _____
2. _____
3. _____
4. _____
5. _____
6. _____

****

Resource Requests:
_____
_____
_____
_____
_____
_____
_____
_____
_____
_____

****

Testing:
_____
_____
_____
_____
_____
_____
_____
_____
_____

****

Trainings/Inservices/Meetings:
_____
_____
_____
_____
_____
_____
_____
_____
_____

FIGURE 7.3
Reading and Resource Weekly Schedule

Where is the Reading Specialist?

Week of _____

Monday	Tuesday	Wednesday	Thursday	Friday

FIGURE 7.4
Example of Completed Weekly Planner

Week of _____Sept. 29th–October 3rd_____

Priorities:
1. Prepare presentation of pretest data for leadership mtg.
2. Order materials for parent reading night
3. Submit proposal for content reading staff development
4. Prepare materials for resource review class
5. Review literacy portfolios of remediation students
6. _____

* *

Resource Requests:
Mrs. Hall – Ideas for fluency development
Ms Westerkamp – novel unit for On My Honor

Mrs. Dowling – novel for lower readers to reinforce social studies unit on
        Great Depression

Mr. Travis – ideas for book reports

Mrs. Dayfield – graphic organizers for teaching bills and amendments in Civics

* *

Testing:
Mustang team requests – Karyn S.
                        Pat H.

Parent request – Janice B. (Lion team)

Child study – Margaret L. (meeting 10/12)

* *

Trainings/Inservices/Meetings:
Leadership Team 3:15–4:15 (9/30)

Reading Specialist Meeting – Friday (10/3)
        – bring curriculum guides and school improvement plan

FIGURE 7.5

FIGURE 7.5
Example of Completed Reading and Resource Weekly Schedule

Where is the Reading Specialist?

Week of _September 29th–October 3rd_

	Monday	Tuesday	Wednesday	Thursday	Friday
7:50–8:25	Resource	Open Lab – Sixth Grade Computer Lab	Resource	Resource	Open Lab – Sixth Grade Computer Lab
1st period	Reading Strat.–Lesson 1 Dolphin Team Rm. 116	Rm. 117	Reading Strat.–Lesson 1 Hawk Team Rm. 109	Rm. 110	VA Young Reader Book Talk 8:25–9:10
2nd period	Resource / Planning (coincides with sixth-grade planning period)				VA Young Reader Book Talk 9:15–10:05
3rd period	Reading Strategies – Lesson 1 Eagle Team Rm. 101	Rm. 102	Rm. 103	Rm. 104	VA Young Reader Book Talk 10:10–11:00
4th period	Reading Strat. – Lesson 2 Cougar Team Rm. 105	Rm. 106			
5th period	Resource / Planning (coincides with seventh-grade planning period)				
6th period	Test Karyn S. Individual Rdg. Inventory 1:10–2:00				Reading Spec. Mtg. – Central Office
7th period	Resource / Planning (coincides with eighth-grade planning period)				1:30–3:30
		School Leadership Meeting 3:15–4:15	Newspaper Info. due!	Resource Review Staff Dev. 3:15–4:15	

Visit teachers to set up times for instruction.

■ Send out an e-mail asking teachers to think about convenient times that you could work with their classes. Include the purpose for your visit and an approximate time frame for how long the lesson should last.

■ Following the e-mail, visit each teacher to schedule specific times to work with classes. Visit teachers during their planning times or before or after school so they are not busy with students.

■ Have your planner and a pack of sticky notes with you. When you decide on a time, write it in your schedule, copy it onto a sticky note, and give it to the teacher. A day or two before you are scheduled to work with a class, stop in the class or e-mail the teacher to confirm your time. If you are presenting a lesson on test-taking strategies, reading strategies, or other vital information, request that the teacher remain in the classroom so he or she can reinforce the concepts that you are teaching.

Organize lesson and staff development materials.

■ For each lesson, label the side and front of a binder with the name of the lesson. I have found this much more effective than trying to keep lessons together in a folder.

■ Organize transparencies for each lesson by placing them in sheet protectors and putting them in binders in the order in which they will be used. You also can place student handouts in sheet protectors and store them in binders for easy reference.

■ When using the same transparency in multiple lessons, make a copy for each binder rather than moving the transparency from one binder to another. For example, in Appendix B you will find a series of reading strategy lessons. Several of the transparencies that appear in the Before Reading lesson are used in the During Reading lesson. Rather than taking them out of the Before Reading Binder, I make duplicates for the During Reading Binder so that the binders remain complete. I have learned that this saves time and prevents you from misplacing materials. I use the same organization system for staff development materials.

■ When copying lessons that the students will be required to keep for future reference (such as those in Appendixes A and B), use paper that has holes or use a three-hole punch to prepare the papers for students. This saves classroom time and allows you to have the students insert the paper into their binders in your presence.

The Reading Specialist Speaks Again: Supporting the Unique Needs of Each Classroom

In order to support classroom instruction, I reiterate the fact that it is important to know the curriculum for each grade level. I suggest familiarizing yourself with the content area textbooks for each grade level so that you can tailor reading strategy instruction to meet teachers' and students' specific needs. In addition, when you work with students in classrooms, you have an opportunity to engage in staff development. You can model teaching techniques, demonstrate how to model strategies for students, and provide the teacher with an opportunity to observe you and classroom interaction.

The needs of each building and each staff will vary greatly, and the reading specialist should have the flexibility and knowledge to develop whatever lessons are requested or required in order to support instruction. There are, however, certain areas that seem to be the focus of many requests for the reading specialist. Reading specialists can use the following suggestions as a starting point as they begin to develop lessons to help support classroom instruction. (See Appendixes A and B for specific materials and instructions for presenting several of these lessons.)

Test-Taking Strategies

I am frequently asked to come in to classrooms and discuss test-taking strategies. In my search for ideas, I came across a system called PIRATES (Hughes, Schumaker, Deshler, & Mercer, 1993)—a mnemonic system designed to help students establish a positive mindset for a test by providing a plan for active thinking. The original PIRATES program is scripted for the instructor and requires significant instructional time for teachers and students to focus intently on each step. I have adapted the PIRATES strategies so they emphasize active thinking during all types of assignments and assessments—not just on end-of-unit or standardized tests—and so that all the steps can be completed in a class period. I also modified the PIRATES strategies to help prepare students for taking a reading test. I present the PIRATES lesson to all sixth-grade classes at the beginning of the school year. (See Appendix A for details and materials for the PIRATES lessons.) Many of the seventh-grade teachers request refresher courses for their students, and it is also presented to eighth-grade reading classes because they are the most involved in standardized testing. It is important for classroom teachers to reinforce the strategies on a daily basis. I have had a tremendous amount of positive feedback from teachers and students about the effectiveness of this particular lesson, and I know that you will, too.

Reading Strategies Lessons

Although I feel that one of the strengths of the reading program at my school is that all sixth- and seventh-grade teachers teach a reading class, it also offers a challenge because many of them, as content area teachers, have little or no background in reading. These teachers are not able to provide students with strategies for active reading because they do not have that information themselves. I originally began developing the following series of lessons so that I could have the opportunity to present reading strategies to all sixth-grade students, but I quickly found that the lessons served a dual purpose in that I also could provide an opportunity for staff development through classroom instruction.

Prior to beginning the series of lessons outlined in Appendix B, meet with the teacher to find out which content area book the students will have available for reference and which chapter they are currently studying. Ask if there are concepts that the students are having particular difficulty with so that you can review and reinforce the information through your lessons. As the reading specialist you also should be aware of any novels that the class is currently reading so that you can refer to them as you demonstrate strategies. Finally, begin scheduling the lessons following the administration of the reading pretest.

Study Skills/Note-Taking

Often teachers become frustrated when their students are not able to read and take notes independently. Rather than simply providing teachers with some ideas, I find the most effective thing to do is to model active reading and learning strategies for the teacher and the students. Initially, I used a reading passage or unit of study that I had selected. However, although some students learned the strategies, others could not make the connection between the "fun activity with the reading specialist" and their content area studies. Thus, I learned that demonstrating effective use of the textbook was best done through the use of the classroom text, not a prepared handout from an unrelated book. Instruction on strategies such as two- and three-column note-taking became far more meaningful to students when we took notes on the current unit of study in social studies or science. In addition, demonstrating how to use a story map was much easier when it was done using a novel that the class was reading.

Concluding Remarks

The key to successful instructional initiatives is to start with a focus on organization and follow with support in the details of implementation. After a schoolwide focus has been established, the staff feels as though they are a part of the focus, and the parents understand the focus. Then reading specialists can begin to develop support from in the classroom, and classroom teachers can begin to develop support from students' homes. We have found that two successful ways of developing support have been through classroom newsletters and posting information on the Internet on the school webpage. We also provide detailed examples of how to support classroom instruction and, based on our experience, what works in the busy day-to-day implementation. We have found that it is crucial for reading specialists to support classroom teachers in a team teaching, modeling capacity. By modeling reading strategy instruction for teachers and sharing in teaching, reading specialists are able to help teachers embrace and take ownership of reading strategy instruction.

CHAPTER 8

Providing Specialized Support for Students and Teachers

"Effective corrective instruction means looking at the big picture and designing complete programs that make the best use of students' time in helping them achieve the goals of proficient reading."

Rasinski & Padak, 2000, p. 211

THIS CHAPTER FOCUSES ON the more traditional aspect of the reading specialist's job—providing specialized support for students in need of assistance. We modify the traditional yearlong pull-out program with short-term, flexible groups, so that all students, even the avid reader and writer, are included.

There may be a time in every student's school career when it may be beneficial to have extra assistance. This may be as short as a one-week intervention for test-taking strategies or as long as a semester for intense reading acceleration. Unfortunately, often the reading specialist is expected to pull out students for daily reading interventions for the student's entire school year, and often these students continue to need extra help year after year (Rasinski & Padak, 2000). And with the advent of high-stakes achievement tests, the challenge continues to "get all students on grade level." Although we do not discuss the inherent fallacies of this approach here (see Allington, 2002, pp. 261–290, for more information on these fallacies), we do offer alternatives to the traditional yearlong "pull-out" program—the expectation and reality for many school-based reading specialists.

Teachers
Administrators
Resources → Parents
Planning and Collaborating With Teachers
Staff Development
Supporting Classroom Instruction
Literacy Program Development and Coordination
Providing Specialized Support
leadership ← instruction
motivation
diagnosis and assessment
Administration and Interpretation
Development and Coordination

Reading Specialists Offer a Variety of Support

Currently, the elementary schools in our district have anywhere from 650 to 980 students attending kindergarten through fifth grade. The middle schools have from 935 students to 1,230 students. These students range from those who are highly motivated and well supported educationally and financially to those who are on free and reduced-cost lunches, sharing homes and resources with extended families, and receiving little home educational support. In addition, enrollment of English-language learners has doubled in the past five years. These students bring to school a wealth of background experiences, but they often lack experiences with school and academic language, narrative print, and standard

English speaking and writing skills. For all students, each school in the district tries to keep in focus three levels of instructional support using small groups: (1) *prevention* to keep students from falling behind, (2) *acceleration* if students are reading one or two levels behind classroom peers, and (3) *long-term support* for students several years behind classroom peers and needing several years of intensive, focused instruction.

Prevention groups may include book clubs, breakfast reading buddies, or whatever the teacher, specialist, and the parents request. Some students may perform with greater confidence and practice when an opportunity arises for them to work in small groups without the classroom peer pressures. Whether a student is in first grade or eighth grade, most students are well aware of the peer group pressures and may relax into learning when he or she has an opportunity for small-group instruction in specific areas of weakness.

For **acceleration** groups, reading specialists in our district offer a variety of small groups in addition to what the students receive in regular classroom instruction. Students may come together to read informational books, practice the writing process, attend to specific vocabulary work or fluency work, or whatever is designated as areas of needs as determined in meetings with classroom teachers. This collaborative style works best when the classroom teacher and the reading specialist share strategies, plan together, and share lessons by exchanging groups. Otherwise, if students are taught different strategies and required to use materials in addition to those they must use in the classroom, they may find it more difficult to understand and negotiate literacy demands instead of accelerating their reading and writing development (Allington, 2001; Allington & Cunningham, 2002).

This shared commitment to the literacy growth of all students is particularly important when students need years of specialized support. Often these students do not receive literacy support at home and many times begin school already "short" on meaningful literacy encounters. For students with little home support, it is imperative that the students enjoy a supportive literacy community at school in order to thrive along with classroom peers. Schools can make a difference in the literacy lives of all students, but struggling students, especially children of poverty who are at risk for school failure, need multiple years of effective instruction if they are to experience success as readers and writers (Allington, 2001; Lipson, Mosenthal, Mekkelsen, & Russ, 2004).

Finally, **long-term support** may require that students work with paraprofessionals, such as a teacher's assistant, twice a week, often for several years, in order to provide students with extra practice time with appropriate adult support. Reading specialists supervise these groups and provide materials, teaching suggestions, and reading strategies, as needed.

The Reading Specialist Speaks: Strengthening Skills Through Specialized Instruction

One of the many joys of being a reading specialist is having the opportunity to work with small groups of students. As educators, we all know that the smaller the student-to-teacher ratio, the more time teachers have to spend with each student. In addition, teachers are better able to individualize instruction, and students are more apt to pay attention because they cannot blend into the scenery. As a former elementary teacher who had classes ranging anywhere from 22 to 32 students during my career, I must say that my first sixth-grade reading group of six students was nirvana. I can still remember their names and faces and the books we read together. I even have a letter in my "keepables" file from one student's mother complimenting me on getting her son excited about reading. Traditionally, these rewarding and beneficial groups were considered the majority of the reading specialist's responsibility. Times have changed, however, and the reading specialist's role is far more global, including not only the struggling readers but also all members of the literacy community. The reading specialist is moving toward a "push-in" as opposed to a pull-out program—the difference being that in a push-in program the reading specialist is more visible in the regular classroom setting and is thereby able to reach more students. While educators are coming to the realization that a schedule strictly consisting of pull-out groups is not the most effective way to reach the maximum number of students, we must keep in mind that specialized instruction does have a place in every reading program. Following are some guidelines for reading specialists to consider as they begin to make decisions about specialized assistance for students and teachers in their buildings. (I also provide some examples of lessons learned so you can avoid making the same mistakes.)

Use assessment results and teacher recommendations to identify students in need of specialized assistance.

Every district or state has specific testing in place to keep track of student progress. As I mentioned in chapter 5, it is important to be familiar with these assessments and be able to interpret their results effectively. When I begin to identify students who may be in need of specialized instruction, I begin with the names of those sixth graders who did not pass or scored poorly on the state standardized reading test in an attempt to intervene early in students' middle school careers. The next piece of information that I have to consider is student performance on the reading pretest that is administered during the first week of school. Then, I confer with the classroom teachers to get their opinions about the students on the list and to find out about other students who they may feel are in need of assistance. I consult the Stafford County Literacy Portfolio, a cumulative record of writing samples, standardized test results, and teacher comments of all students in kindergarten through eighth grade, to see if any of the students have previously received the services of a reading specialist or if teachers have made comments about specific areas of weakness related to literacy. Using all these pieces of information helps me paint a better portrait of the reader than solely relying on standardized test data. I keep a cumulative data sheet in my planning binder as I gather this information, which allows me to identify common student needs. Figure 8.1 illustrates how a comprehensive data sheet can allow you to identify groups in need of special attention and plan for appropriate instruction. For example, based on the information on this data sheet, I was able to place students in one of four groups, depending on their specific needs. Table 8.1 shows the focus of each group and the students placed in each group.

Create a plan to meet the needs of each group.

Although I follow the same format with the reading strategies and test-taking strategies lessons that I do in whole-class settings, what goes on in small groups is very different. Each group of students is unique. Teaching exactly the same thing in exactly the same way to every group that comes through your door takes the "special" out of specialized instruction. Some groups of students are good at decoding words and have a well-developed sight vocabulary but lack the active reading skills necessary for comprehension. Other groups have strong comprehension skills but are hindered by a lack of fluency and word recognition. Still other groups need help with every aspect of the reading process. In order to create a plan for each group, the reading specialist must have a variety of techniques, programs, and materials to choose from and be able to use them all effectively.

FIGURE 8.1
Cumulative Student Data Sheet

Name	SOL 400=pass	Rdg.Pretest IndepRdgLvl	Literacy Portfolio	Teacher Recommendations	Additional Information
Beth	365	5	Special ed.services 1st-3rd	good vocab; fluent reader; poor comp.	
Anna	395	4	comp.weak 4th/5th	concentrate on rdg.for maning	
Roger	360	3.6	new to county	poor fluency slow comp.	shy, quiet
Donna	378	4.6	weak organiz. 4th/5th	work on org., study skills, testing	
Chris	392	5	loves to read	work on study skills; test strat.	
Judi	375	4.2	rdg. specialist services 4th	work on decoding/fluency	
John	350	3.5	" " 4th/5th	weak vocab. and comp.	
Maria	350	3.6	" " 5th	struggles with rdg.	English is second lang.
Stacy	375	4	motivated; hardworker	difficulty reading fluently	
Tony	385	4	new to county	vocab + decoding ok; poor comp & fluency	
David	395	5	positive comments K-5th	weak org, study skills; test strat.	
Jeff	360	3.5	rdg. specialist serv. 4th	low vocab./low comp.	
Louise	365	3.6	special ed. services K-3rd	struggles with vocab & comp. *comp.	Individual Reading Inventory - 2nd-4th
Lauren	390	5	very motivated	test-taking strat.; study help	
Bill	357	3.5	new to county	calls words/ needs help with comprehension	
Lou	405	4.4	new to county	comprehension weak	
Janey	403	4.2	new to county	comp/vocab. good- work on fluency	good decoding
Tom	408	4	comp. issues rated K-5th	comp skills appear weak	
Erin	405	6.5	very social;needs focus	organization/study skills	parents supportive

108

TABLE 8.1
Specialized Groups Formed From Data Sheet

Group 1—Focus on comprehension and fluency
    Judi
    Tony
    Jeff
    Janey

Group 2—Focus on active reading strategies and comprehension
    Beth
    Anna
    Bill
    Lou
    Tom

Group 3—Focus on organization, study skills, and test-taking strategies using content area materials
    Donna
    Chris
    Stacy
    David
    Lauren
    Erin

Group 4—Focus on vocabulary building and basic reading skills
    John
    Louise
    Maria
    Roger

Collaborate with the classroom teacher to create a smooth transition out of and back into the classroom.

Constant communication with the classroom teacher is a must when taking students out of the classroom for specialized instruction. For example, if a class is in the middle of reading a novel, I incorporate that novel into my instruction. If a class starts a new novel while a student is with me, I make sure that the student has the information necessary to jump in and continue on with the class. Reading specialists should be careful not to create situations in which students are more confused or in which they are left behind.

Reading specialists also need to use a common vocabulary in the area of reading. Too often struggling readers are taken out of the classroom and put into a highly structured reading program in which specific terminology and vocabulary are used. If the vocabulary used by the reading specialist is not carried over in the regular classroom and vice versa, students will not make the connection between the strategies and skills that they worked on with the reading specialist and their daily instruction in the classroom. For example, during my first year at Thompson Middle School, I coordinated the Learning Through Listening program at our school. This program was targeted for our special education students who had books on tape written as an accommodation on their Individualized Education Plan and also for students who were dyslexic, visually impaired, or had significant difficulty with print. We had an account with Recordings for the Blind and Dyslexic, had purchased four-track tape players, and had the tapes for the social studies and science text books, as well as novels that the students would be using in reading class. I spent hours training small groups of students to use the four-track tape players. I had the parents sign forms taking responsibility for the machines so they could be taken home and I even created a system where the students could come to me to get the tapes that they needed. You can imagine my disappointment when I saw how little this program was used in the classroom and in students' homes. However, it was a learning experience (as illustrated in the Reading and Resource Evaluation Chart in Figure 2.4, page 19). I realized that the only way this program could be implemented effectively was for the content area teachers or special education case manager to be the person who trained the students and followed up on their use of the program. I also realized that the program used up a lot of my time, so it would be more effective to run the program through the special education department.

Be available to offer specialized assistance to teachers.
Reading specialists understand the relationship between effective reading instruction and student achievement. In order to make sure students understand the content area, reading specialists guide them through the text, provide materials at an appropriate reading level, and assist with text that it too difficult. However, as previously mentioned in chapter 1, teacher preparation in teaching reading can vary from as many as 24 hours of semester work to as little as 3 hours. This means that many schools will have teachers who are in need of specialized assistance in teaching reading or in content area reading strategies.

The nature of the reading program at Thompson Middle School offered me a great opportunity to interact with the majority of teachers in the building. All the sixth- and seventh-grade teachers came to me for resources and trade books for their reading classes. Many of them were familiar only with their content area and had never taught reading, so they were quick to seek assistance and advice. This was the perfect opportunity to offer to come to their classroom and teach a unit together or to provide resources that would help them strengthen the content area reading of their students. I learned quickly during my first year that I should never assume that someone is an experienced reading teacher or that he or she knows how to effectively use materials without guidance. For example, a special education teacher came to me quite often seeking materials and ideas for her students who were reading approximately four to five years below grade level. She was enthusiastic and excited about teaching, wanted to do the best she could for her students, and seemed like an experienced teacher. I provided her with materials, sent her to a training session, and offered lots of ideas. She would listen to my explanations, ask questions, take the material, and, to the best of my knowledge, use it successfully. About midway through the school year, she came to me completely frustrated because her students were not demonstrating reading progress and they lacked motivation. It was then that I realized that she had no prior experience teaching reading and that instead of handing her the materials, I needed to show her how to use them. We planned a unit together. I spent two weeks in the reading class modeling teaching strategies and team teaching, and the results were positive: The students became engaged in the novel, began participating actively in class activities, and showed a desire to read more novels. The teacher had a much better understanding of how to reach her students, and I learned a valuable lesson about the responsibilities of my job.

Concluding Remarks

This chapter discussed the challenge of providing support for all students and extra assistance to those students who struggle with one or more aspects of literacy learning. Again, we underscored the need for flexibility in the implementation of this part of the reading specialist's job. What is beneficial for one teacher may not be necessary for another teacher, and what is necessary for one group of students may not be at all what another group needs. Some students may actually regress when pulled out for intervention, especially if they miss reading time in the classroom or perceive that they are less capable than their classroom peers. Thus, we do not give prescriptions, but instead offer suggestions for providing support and urge each reading specialist to work within the needs of his or her school.

CHAPTER 9

Motivating the Literacy Community

"Those who do not develop the pleasure reading habit simply don't have a chance—they will have a very difficult time reading and writing at a level high enough to deal with the demands of today's world."

Krashen, 2004, p. x

W E HAVE ADDED THE idea of motivation to the center of the literacy program model graphic. We feel that motivation is perhaps the most important aspect of a literacy program. Why do we feel this way? Because, as noted in a study by Gambrell, Dromsky, and Mazzoni (2000), most teachers, when asked, describe reading motivation as one of the biggest challenges they face. It is often especially difficult at the intermediate or middle school level to motivate students to read because of students' awareness of peer pressure and their growing involvement in extracurricular activities (Oldfather, 1995).

Whether reading is required to complete class assignments or for pleasure, struggling students often perceive reading as a boring, painful process, and an activity to be avoided at all costs. The very students who need additional practice with print, those who routinely suffer from the "Matthew effect" (Stanovich, 1986, p. 381) of endless worksheets and little exposure to print, present the greatest challenge. Stanovich (1986) also describes the phenomena of struggling students who endure many worksheets assigned by well-meaning teachers and assistants to "fix" their literacy weaknesses, yet what the students are really lacking is sustained engagement with print. The very students who need the free reading time the most, because their homes may not have the resources to provide interesting, appropriate free reading material, are the students who often experience the least time in the school day for this important foundational activity. For these and all students, free reading time is critical for reading growth and motivation.

It follows then that illiteracy is not as pervasive a problem as is aliteracy—and a negative attitude toward reading, which often develops due to a lack of reading practice (Beers, 1998; Mathewson, 1994). However, when the literacy team meets with the principal and other teachers in the building, schedules, class requirements, and personnel issues tend to take precedence over reading time, resource availability, and staff expertise.

Teachers   Administrators

Resources   → Parents

Planning and Collaborating With Teachers

Staff Development

Supporting Classroom Instruction

Literacy Program Development and Coordination

Providing Specialized Support

leadership ⟷ instruction

motivation

diagnosis and assessment

Administration and Interpretation

Development and Coordination

Teachers as Readers, Teachers of Reading

Whether a student is proficient or struggling with literacy demands, the issue remains that without exercising literacy skills, the student will not improve. The coach of a sport recognizes the importance of practice to build proficiency, and parents recognize the necessity of sports practice, yet literacy skills often are practiced only when required for a grade or classroom project. Reading is rarely done for fun, practice, or for aesthetic reasons. The challenge remains to help students gain a deep appreciation for literacy, while developing literacy skills for life. Au (1993) suggests that the very definition of literacy involves ability as well as willingness to use reading and writing to construct meaning.

Teachers must show students, on a daily basis, how reading can be rewarding. Teachers must honestly view independent reading as a valuable learning activity, for their students and for themselves, or the students will not "buy in" to the free reading time with enthusiasm. Reading and writing enjoyment often depends on classroom teachers' abilities to provide students with opportunities and time to read and write about what they find interesting and meaningful (Winograd & Paris, 1988–1989). If teachers do not enjoy reading for pleasure, it becomes difficult for them to convince their students to read for enjoyment. Teachers cannot fool students; students know if a teacher walks around with books, newspapers, or magazines, or only accesses print in classroom texts (Beers, 2003; Ogle, 2002). For example, a physical education teacher I observed at the middle level did his bus duty every morning with a paperback book in his hand. He would fill the time between buses by reading his book and sharing reading recommendations and ideas with students as they walked into school. He set a powerful example of literacy enjoyment to each student at the beginning of each day.

Reading Growth Requires Time to Read— for Students and Teachers

At the beginning of every year, it is exciting and rewarding to see teachers come into the building carrying the latest adolescent or children's literature that they "discovered" over the summer. It has been our experience that once a teacher connects to a book and enjoys reading it, the teacher becomes "hooked" and naturally shares this connection with students, as well as other teachers.

To encourage wide independent reading by our teachers, the school district sponsors several "Teachers as Readers" seminars throughout the summer months and throughout the school year. The purpose of these seminars is to read and discuss popular children's and adolescent literature. This past year, these seminars were so popular that many schools opted to have their own: Many faculties organized Teachers as Readers breakfast groups, after-school socials, and even a Teachers as Readers happy hour—complete with root beer and popcorn. When teachers have the opportunity and resources provided so they can choose, read, and discuss books, they become avid readers and are more eager to share their enthusiasm with their students. As part of the seminar, teachers are required to complete a book advertisement and think of one or two essential questions to ask students while reading the book. Teachers share their advertisements and questions with one another so all participants can benefit from them. Teachers receive staff development points toward recertification for attending these sessions, and they comment that the resource knowledge they gain is beneficial for enriching the independent and group reading in their classrooms.

Our local bookstore even participates by offering teacher discounts on books they want to purchase for classroom use, as well as by reserving a space in the store each week for book discussions. (See Figure 9.1

FIGURE 9.1
Teachers as Readers Invitation

Joins us for a

Teachers as Readers
Discussion Group
Read the Virginia Young Readers selections for this coming year
and discuss teaching ideas with colleagues
We will meet at The Scholarship, Aquia Towne Center, where we
will receive a discount on any Virginia Young Reader book
purchased.
We will carry on book discussions in the
bookstore reception area.
Primary, intermediate, middle and high school
selections available.
2:30 - 3:45 PM
Tuesday,
July 6, 13, 20, 27

for a sample invitation to a Teachers as Readers event.) Parents often join book discussions and bring their children, too. The popularity of the seminars and independent reading selections continues to expand. It has been our experience that reading skills without the desire to read independently often results in skill atrophy, perhaps causing parents to think their child has a reading problem, when he or she actually has a reading practice problem.

Literacy Celebrations

Similar to an athletic coach organizing sports banquets and awards ceremonies to celebrate the athletic community, the reading specialist—often working with the media specialist—organizes and promotes literacy celebrations throughout the school year. Whether in elementary, middle, or high school, literacy celebrations can highlight the enjoyment and importance of literacy in everyday life. Although the building principal is responsible for the schoolwide vision and school plan for literacy instruction, someone needs to be responsible for planning, organizing, and supervising literacy events. Therefore, most building administrators welcome the assistance of the reading specialist, serving as the school's literacy coach, to continually promote and coordinate schoolwide literacy events.

Honors for Literacy Achievements

As part of a reading incentive program, every year each school in the district tries to recognize and honor readers in creative ways, similar to aspiring athletes, artists, and authors. Students, parents, and teachers look forward to the accompanying celebrations and work to earn honors throughout the school year. These incentives help successful readers expand their literary knowledge, and they help reluctant readers get involved in reading. Often siblings come to orientation at the middle school level, eager to know if they will have the same opportunity for reading incentives that their older siblings enjoyed.

I recently attended a Poetry Café at one of our previously lower achieving middle schools where students were recognized for their accomplishments by staff, their peers, and parents. Sixth-, seventh-, and eighth-grade students were dressed up: young men in dress pants, ironed shirts, and ties and stylish young women in dresses and heels. These young men and women were at school in the evening with family members to read their original poetry—some even had designed professional-looking PowerPoint presentations. The school orchestra played background music as the family-living classes served homemade hors d'oeuvres and punch. That evening, all participants acted as contributing members of the schoolwide literacy community, a community that encompassed parents, teachers, and school board members.

I also attended the Super Readers Luncheon at one of our Title I elementary schools. Young readers achieving the highest distinction possible, reading all 12 of the Virginia Young Readers books at their grade levels independently and completing book talks on books of their choice for their classmates, earned an invitation to the literary luncheon in the media center. At the special luncheon, students are surprised by a visit from a therapy dog from PAWS for Reading, a program designed to pair service dogs with children who are learning to read. Another school rents a limousine service, and with permission from parents, students are picked up at their homes after school and taken to the local fast food restaurant of their choice. Then they are driven around their neighborhoods, so they can wave at friends and family members.

The Reading Specialist Speaks: Thoughtful Reading Incentives

Although organization has always been a personal challenge, motivation to read has never been an issue for me. The mere sight of a book is motivation for me to read, but unfortunately that is not the case for many students. Teacher motivation plays a critical role in student attitude and achievement, which is why the first five chapters of this book are dedicated to suggestions for creating positive, collaborative, and cooperative relationships between reading specialists and members of the literacy team.

Regardless of how well organized or exciting a reading incentive is, it can be successful only with the support and cooperation of the entire literacy community. If parents are not aware that a reading incentive is available, if teachers are not willing to promote and encourage students to take part in the incentive, or if administrative support is not present, incentives will only reach a minimal number of students. Reading incentives may be simple or elaborate, and they may involve individual or team effort. Rewards may vary from a pencil to a pizza party to the principal parachuting from a plane. The Reading and Resource Evaluation

Chart in Table 2.4 (see page 19) can be helpful in developing a reading incentive and then examining its effectiveness. Although the reading incentives offered in the elementary and middle schools in Stafford County are too numerous to describe, I would like to share two schoolwide incentives that have helped to promote literacy at my school.

Summer Reading Incentive

The summer reading incentive is the result of a cooperative effort between the media specialists and me, the reading specialist. We created a summer reading list of approximately 35 to 40 books for each grade level; it included a variety of genres and reading levels. Our objective is twofold: (1) We provide the parents and students with suggestions for titles rather than simply saying, "Be sure to read over the summer!" and (2) we send a clear message to the families coming to our school that reading is a priority. Each list (see Figure 9.2 for a sample reading list) is sent home accompanied by a letter (see Figure 9.3), which explains the importance of continuing to practice reading skills over the summer and describes how the students can receive their incentive reward in September. A blank book review form (see Figure 9.4, page 122) is copied on the back of the letter. Once the lists and letters are copied and ready for distribution, I take the following steps to ensure the incentive is well promoted. The various members of the literacy community involved are noted in bold print.

- During the sixth-grade **parent** orientation in May, I talk about the outstanding reading program in our school, distribute and discuss the summer reading incentive, and invite parents to volunteer in the reading resource room or library.

- When the **rising sixth graders** arrive in our building for their orientation (usually a few days after the parent orientation), I speak to them about the reading program and encourage them to participate in the summer incentive.

- I deliver the letter and summer reading list (see pages 120–121) to the **elementary reading specialists** who, in turn, distribute them to the students.

- **Homeroom teachers** are asked to distribute the list to **rising seventh and eighth graders** prior to their last day of school. Then, either the **media specialist** or the **reading specialist** can make announcements about the incentive to these students.

FIGURE 9.2
Sample Reading List

Thompson Middle School
Summer 2004 Suggested Reading List for
Rising Seventh Graders

(F) = Fiction
(NF) = Nonfiction
(VYR) = Virginia Young Reader 2004-2005

Avi. DON'T YOU KNOW THERE'S A WAR ON? Set in Brooklyn, New York in 1943, this novel follows the lives of eleven-year-old Howie Crispers and his best friend Denny. Each boy's father is a soldier serving time during World War II. When the boys hear their teacher, Miss Gossim, is in danger of being fired they set out to "save" her. (F)

Bauer, Joan. HOPE WAS HERE. Hope is on the move again, relocating from New York to a job as a waitress at the Welcome Staircase Diner in Wisconsin. There she finds herself in the midst of a small town scandal and a wonderful group of new friends. (F)

Bradley, Kimberly Brubaker. HALFWAY TO THE SKY. After her brother dies and her parents get a divorce, twelve-year-old Katahdin sets out to hike the whole Appalachian Trail from Georgia to Maine on her own. (F) (VYR)

Blumberg, Rhoda. SHIPWRECKED: THE TRUE ADVENTURES OF A JAPANESE BOY. This biography focuses on the adventures of Manjiro, a young fisherman growing up in 19th century Japan. By law any person who leaves the shores of Japan may not return under penalty of death. Despite the threat, Manjiro takes the chance to return to his homeland. (NF)

Bridges, Ruby. THROUGH MY EYES. Ruby Bridges tells the moving story of her year as a 1st grade student at the all-white William Frantz Public School in New Orleans in 1960. (NF)

Cannon, Ann Edwards. CHARLOTTE'S ROSE. As a twelve-year-old Welsh immigrant carries a motherless baby along the Mormon Trail in 1856, she comes to love the baby as her own and fear the day the baby's father will reclaim her. (F) (VYR)

Carbone, Elisa. STORM WARRIORS. This novel relates, in authentic detail, the sea rescue methods used by an African-American lifesaving crew on Pea Island, NC in the late eighteen hundreds. (F)

Choldenk, Gennifer. NOTES FROM A LIAR AND HER DOG. Ant (Antonia) believes she is the unloved middle daughter. She takes refuge from reality in her vivid imagination and in her friendships with her best friend Harrison and her dog Pistachio. However, she actually begins to believe her fantasies and cannot stop herself from lying. (F)

Coleman, Penny. ROSIE THE RIVETER. This book tells how World War II brought about extraordinary job opportunities for women. On the home front, businesses employed women as men filled the military ranks. (NF)

Cushman, Karen. MATILDA BONE. Fourteen-year-old Matilda, apprentice bonesetter in a medieval English village, tries to reconcile the spiritual and practical aspects of her life. (F)

Farmer, Nancy. THE EAR, THE EYE, AND THE ARM. General Malslkas' three children "escape" their fortress home, are kidnapped by She Elephant, and are forced to mine plastic from the 20th century. Three mutant detectives are hired to use their special powers to find them. (F)

Fenner, Carol. YOLANDA'S GENIUS. Genius is not just book learning, as Yolanda discovers when she realizes her brother has a gift for music. (F)

Freedman, Russell. LINCOLN: A PHOTOBIOGRAPHY. This award-winning book traces the life of Abraham Lincoln through the medium of photojournalism. (NF)

French, Jackie. HITLER'S DAUGHTER. After hearing a fictional tale about Hitler's daughter, Mark, an Australian boy, wonders what it would be like if someone he loved and trusted turned out to be evil. (F) (VYR)

Giff, Patricia Reilly. PICTURES OF HOLLIS WOODS. A troublesome twelve-year-old orphan, staying with an elderly artist who needs her, remembers the only other time she was happy in a foster home, with a family that truly seemed to care about her. (F) (VYR)

Godfrey, Neale. ULTIMATE KID'S MONEY BOOK. This book has everything you need to know about money – how to earn, save, spend and share it. (NF)

Greene, Bette. SUMMER OF MY GERMAN SOLDIER. The summer that Patty Bergen turns 12 is a summer that will haunt her forever. When her small hometown in Arkansas becomes the site of a prison camp housing German soldiers, Patty learns what it means to open her heart. Even though she's Jewish, she begins to see prison escapee, Anton, not as a Nazi, but as a lonely, frightened young man with feelings not unlike her own. Patty risks losing family, friends -- even her freedom -- for this dangerous friendship. (F)

Haddix, Margaret Peterson. JUST ELLA. Ella finds that accepting Prince Charming's proposal catches her in a dull world of needlework and etiquette. As she comes to believe her prince is really Prince Boring, she plots her escape. (F)

Hobbs, Will. RIVER THUNDER. Jessie, Troy, and the rest of the crew from DOWNRIVER have returned to the Grand Canyon for adventure on the Colorado River. In the year since they last were together, each has changed; each feels more mature, but how will they interact now that they are facing new challenges-challenges greater than anything they've had to deal with at home? (F)

Holt, Kimberly Willis. DANCING IN CADILLAC LIGHT. In 1968, eleven-year-old Jaynell's life in the town of Moon, Texas, is enlivened when her eccentric Grandpap comes to live with her family. (F)(VYR)

FIGURE 9.3
Summer Reading Incentive Letter

May 10, 2004

Dear Parents:

Summer is almost here! We are sure your child's head is filled with visions of long-awaited vacations, trips to the pool, and days full of freedom from school and assignments. Those are all important, but we urge you to make sure that your child also continues to read regularly throughout the break. Just like athletic skills, reading skills need to be practiced consistently or they become rusty and more difficult to revive in September.

In order to help encourage reading we are providing a list of suggested books for our eighth-grade students. When your child arrives at Thompson in September he or she can receive recognition and a goody-bag by completing one of the following activities for the book(s) that they have read:

- discuss the book with one of us
- take and pass an Accelerated Reader test on the book
- write a summary of the book using the form on the back of this letter

They will also have the opportunity to get a head start on the Virginia Young Readers Program. All students who read four or more of the Virginia Young Reader titles and successfully complete one of the above listed criteria for each book get to participate in a pizza party sponsored by the Thompson Parent–Teacher Organization.

At Thompson Middle School, we realize that reading is the key to learning and we ask that you support us by encouraging your child to read and by reading with them. If you have any questions please feel free to give us a call. Thank you for being a part of our educational team.

Sincerely,
Stephanie Pettengill   Eileen Godwin
Reading Specialist   Media Specialist

Tammie Grayson   Lisa Whitt
Media Specialist   Media Center Assistant

■ Summer reading lists for each grade level are copied and placed in the main office and **guidance office** so that students who register over the summer have the opportunity to participate. Copies of the summer reading list also can be sent to any **local public libraries** where students might visit over the summer.

■ Prior to the arrival of students at the beginning of the school year, **student or parent volunteers** prepare goody-bags as reading incentives. Each bag includes treats (chocolate and nonchocolate items),

FIGURE 9.4
Summer Reading Incentive Book Review

Thompson Middle School Summer Reading Incentive
Book Review

Name: _____ Date: _____
Title: _____
Author/Illustrator: _____
Setting: _____
Characters: _____
_____

Summary: _____
_____
_____
_____
_____
_____
_____
_____
_____
_____
_____
_____
_____
_____
_____
_____
_____
_____
_____
_____
_____

bookmarks, pencils, items with motivational messages, and a 25-cent coupon to the school store. The coupons are sponsored by the **Parent–Teacher Organization**. I load these bags on a rolling cart for easy transportation to classrooms.

▪ Then, I create a schedule for distributing the incentive rewards. Figure 9.5 shows the distribution schedule that I have found effective for the middle school. On the first day of school, announcements are made to share this schedule with the students. I do not accept or distribute anything related to the summer reading program on the first day of school, so teachers will have minimal disruptions during the hectic day. Eighth graders, many of whom have participated already in previous years and are familiar with the building, are asked to report to me first, while the sixth graders, who are still adjusting to the organization and enormity of the middle school, are given a few reminders and a few days to learn their way around. I always make sure I create the distribution schedule in advance with the classroom teachers so that instruction is not interrupted.

■ I document students' names and homerooms when they successfully complete the summer reading program through turning in their completed book review forms, giving an acceptable oral summary, or taking an Accelerated Reader test. I usually post the names in a central location in the building and (depending on the number of students who participate) send them to the **local newspaper**. In addition, further recognition or rewards can be given to those grade levels or homerooms with the highest participation.

FIGURE 9.5
Sample Distribution Schedule

Welcome to a new school year. Your cooperation in distributing the Summer Reading Incentive letters and lists in June was greatly appreciated. It is now time to reward the participants of this incentive for a job well done—and to see how many of our Jaguars did some reading over the summer. I would like to distribute awards using the following schedule:

Tuesday, September 3rd
Schedule will be read during morning announcements.

Wednesday, September 4th
Eighth-grade students report to the upstairs computer lab during homeroom period.

Thursday, September 5th
Seventh-grade students report to the downstairs computer lab during homeroom period.

Friday, September 6th
Dolphin and Cougar teams report to the downstairs computer lab during homeroom period. Falcon, Eagle, and Lion teams report at the beginning of first period. Hawk and Panther teams report at the beginning of fourth period.

Monday, September 9th
Last chance for all students! Students can report to the downstairs computer lab during homeroom.

Thank you for your cooperation. Please let me know if you have any questions or need to schedule a different time.

◾ In the past, we began revising and editing the lists for the coming school year in April. We added the new books from the Virginia Young Readers Program and deleted books that were not widely read. This year, the media specialists and the reading specialists worked collaboratively to create a district list for each grade level.

This summer reading program is well worth the time and effort because it involves all of the members of the literacy community: The feeder elementary schools, the guidance office staff, the Parent–Teacher Organization, the administration, and the school faculty are all active and essential parts of the success of the program. In addition, the sixth-grade students arrive at the middle school seeking out the reading specialist and media specialist—key personnel in their literary success.

Virginia Young Readers Program

Each year a committee from the Virginia State Reading Association works hard to select outstanding contributions to literature for the Virginia Young Readers Program. These are books that have been deemed noteworthy in the field of children's or young adult literature; have been in print less than five years; and have been nominated by media specialists, teachers, students, or other member of the literacy community. From these nominations, 10 books are selected at the primary, elementary, middle, and high school levels. These books are used as the basis for a yearly reading incentive in our school because they are thoroughly reviewed, thoughtfully selected, and represent a variety of genres and student interests. While educators in Virginia are fortunate enough to have these books already selected, the literacy team in any school could meet to decide upon an appropriate list of titles to implement a similar program. The Virginia Young Readers Program is handled differently in each school in our district, based on the needs of the staff and students. Each year, the program is implemented at my school as follows:

◾ After identifying the titles for the next school year (usually done in early April), we purchase multiple copies of each title to keep in the media center. The Parent–Teacher Organization supports this incentive by purchasing approximately half of the books; the remainder of the titles are purchased with school funds. We estimate the number of students who will participate in the incentive based on the previous year's actual number. Then, the estimated number of students participating in the incentive is used to determine the number of titles we purchase. In

124

addition, these titles are included on each of the summer incentive reading lists so students have the opportunity to get an early start.

■ We dedicate a wall in the media center to documenting student progress in the program. Charts that help track individual progress (see Figure 9.6 for an example) can be prepared by the media specialist, reading specialist, or volunteer and posted on the wall.

■ At the end of September, the media specialists and I meet to develop a plan for a book talk as a way of introducing the books on the lists to students. We discuss connections between the books on the list and decide who will be responsible for presenting each title during the

---

FIGURE 9.6
Virginia Young Reader Progress Chart

Virginia Young Reader
2003-2004

Name _____

Grade _____ Team _____

A Single Shard by Linda Sue Park	_____
Don't You Know There's a War Going On? by Avi	_____
Flipped by Wendelin Van Draanen	_____
Lord of the Deep by Graham Salisbury	_____
Lord of the Nutcracker Men by Iain Lawrence	_____
Notes From a Liar and Her Dog by Gennifer Choldenko	_____
Savion: My Life in Tap by Savion Glover	_____
Shipwrecked: The True Adventures of a Japanese Boy by Rhoda Blumberg	_____
Storm Warriors by Elisa Carbone	_____
The Last Book in the Universe by Rodman Philbrick	_____

book talk. Then, teachers receive a copy of the program guidelines (see Figure 9.7), and book talks are scheduled for all sixth- through eighth-grade classes in the media center. (See Figure 9.8 for an example of a book talk sign-up sheet.)

FIGURE 9.7
Reading Incentive Guidelines for Teachers

Dear Literacy Team Members:
It is time to begin the Virginia Young Readers Program. All students will be eligible to participate and we are looking forward to lots of participation. The following is a list of the titles that have been selected for the 2001–2002 school year:

At Her Majesty's Request, Walter Dean Myers   *Bat 6*, Virginia Wolff
Blackwater, Eve Bunting   *Bodies from the Bog*, James Deem
Dave at Night, Gail Carson Levine   *Downsiders*, Neil Shusterman
Ghost in the Tokaido Inn, Dorothy Hoobler   *Speed of Light*, Sybil Rosen

The Great Turkey Walk, Kathleen Karr
When Zachary Beaver Came to Town, Kimberly Holt

Here is how the program will work:
1. You sign up for a time for us to come into your classes to do a book talk. You can decide as a team how this is done so that we have a chance to meet with all of your students. We will give the book talks from October 15th to October 26th. A sign-up sheet will be posted in the workrooms.
2. When a student finishes reading a book, he or she does one of the following:
   • takes an Accelerated Reader test and turns in the results to us
   • conferences with one of us to discuss the book
   • writes a summary of the book (there will be a short standard form provided) and turns it in to us
3. After successfully completing step 2, students will be given a progress chart. They will write their name and team on it and we will initial beside each book the student has completed. These charts will be displayed in the library.
4. On March 1st, students who have read four or more of the books will vote on the their favorite title of the 2000–2001 school year during a pizza party. The winning title will be announced that afternoon.
5. Top readers will receive awards and all participants will receive a certificate.

As you can see, this program requires very little effort on your part. Hooray! All we ask is that between now and October 12th you sign up for a book talk, encourage the children to read, and allow them to visit one of us upon the completion of a book. You may choose to use one of the titles as a read-aloud or as part of a literature circle...as long as the children successfully demonstrate comprehension, they are given credit.
   We are really excited about kicking this program off and hope that you share our enthusiasm. If you have any questions or suggestions, you know where to find us!

Happy Reading,
Stephanie Pettengill, Reading Specialist
Eileen Godwin, Media Specialist
Tammie Grayson, Media Specialist

FIGURE 9.8
Book Talk Sign-Up Sheet

Virginia Young Readers Book Talks
Mrs. Godwin, Mrs. Grayson, and Mrs. Pettengill

Monday, October 15th

1st period _____
2nd period _____
5th period _____
6th period _____
7th period _____

Tuesday, October 16th

1st period _____
2nd period _____
5th period _____
6th period _____
7th period _____

Wednesday, October 17th

1st period _____
2nd period _____
5th period _____
6th period _____
7th period _____

Thursday, October 18th

1st period _____
2nd period _____
5th period _____
6th period _____
7th period _____

Monday, October 22nd

6th period _____
7th period _____

Tuesday, October 23rd

6th period _____
7th period _____

Virginia Young Readers Book Talks
Mrs. Godwin, Mrs. Grayson, and Mrs. Pettengill

Wednesday, October 17th

3rd period _____
4th period _____

Thursday, October 18th

3rd period _____
4th period _____

Monday, October 22nd

1st period _____
2nd period _____
3rd period _____
4th period _____
5th period _____

Tuesday, October 23rd

1st period _____
2nd period _____
3rd period _____
4th period _____
5th period _____

Wednesday, October 24nd

1st period _____
2nd period _____
3rd period _____
4th period _____
5th period _____

Thursday, October 25th

1st period _____
2nd period _____
3rd period _____
4th period _____
5th period _____

- Upon arrival at the book talk, each student receives a bookmark with the featured titles listed on it. Then, we explain the guidelines of the program to the students: Students who read four or more of the books will be eligible to attend a pizza party, will vote for their favorite title of the year, and will receive a certificate of recognition. Students who read all 10 titles will receive additional rewards and recognition. Previous rewards have included donated gift certificates from local merchants, books from the next year's Virginia Young Readers list, and homework passes. Students receive credit for reading a book in the same ways as the summer reading incentive: by presenting an oral or written summary or passing an Accelerated Reader test.

- As students successfully demonstrate that they have read and comprehended one of the books, the media specialist or reading specialist signs off on the appropriate line on the individual progress chart. After a student has read all 10 titles, his or her name is written on a cutout in the shape of the state of Virginia and placed in a designated space on the wall.

- Throughout the course of the program—which runs from October through the end of February—periodic announcements are made about the progress of the program, book talks are conducted, and excerpts from the books are read over the morning announcements by students or faculty members.

- A pizza party is held for qualifying students in March as a part of our Read Across America celebration. During the party, students have the opportunity to discuss the books and vote for their favorite. A tally of their votes is sent to the state committee and a few weeks later the winning title for the state is reported.

- Certificates and rewards are distributed at the awards ceremony at the end of the school year. The current participants then become the first to receive a list of the books that the committee has chosen for the following year.

The program began in the 2000–2001 school year with about 12 participants. In the 2004–2005 school year, we had 97 participants. Although the participants were initially students who were avid readers, each year more and more average and reluctant readers became a part of the Virginia Young Readers Program. Because the goal of reading four books in five months seemed attainable to students and many of our teachers encouraged student participation by using one of the titles as a read-aloud, reluctant readers received the extra push they needed to participate. I also offered a staff development class in which I discussed the Virginia Young Readers Program with staff members, shared the titles that had been selected for the next school year, and allowed staff members to choose a title to read and create a poster or advertisement for it. The results were great: Participants in the class included math teachers, geography teachers, a teacher of multi-handicapped students, science teachers, and even an orchestra teacher. They created original, informative, and intriguing posters that helped promote the program and reinforce the message to the students that every teacher is a reading teacher and that they are part of a literacy community.

Concluding Remarks

Everyone benefits from a collaborative, motivated literacy community in which students, parents, administrators, and teachers work together to enjoy reading and writing opportunities. Evidence of this motivated literacy community occurs when siblings of students attending the middle school enter and ask when they can participate in the Virginia Young Readers Program, or when teachers outside our school ask if they can attend one of our staff development sessions. In addition to creating a motivated literacy community, standardized test scores continue to rise in the area of English and reading, as well as in the content areas of science and history. The most rewarding benefit, however, continues to be the thank-yous teachers receive from parents when their children actually ask to go to the library—for fun. It takes a community to support a literate child.

Conclusion

THERE ARE CERTAIN CHARACTERISTICS necessary to be a leader and productive change agent in the area of literacy instruction. Individuals need leadership skills, such as courage of conviction, and a comprehensive knowledge of reading research, materials, strategies, and children's literature to share with others. Individuals also need interpersonal skills to be an effective literacy leader and collaborator. Finally, successful literacy leaders need to understand that change works best when it is supported by those in the community and in the school and thus work to get the community involved in literacy efforts.

In order to stay informed on the different aspects of the reading program throughout the district, I visit one school each week. Recently, I visited a middle school that prides itself in celebrating reading and readers. At the time the middle school was featuring an author visit, and I was eager to hear the author whom the school had invited. As a class, all sixth-grade students had read and discussed one of the author's books. Every sixth-grade student was invited, with his or her academic team (i.e., each content area teacher on the team), to come to the media center and listen to an hour-long presentation by the author about writing her books. Students had the opportunity to ask questions regarding writing, plot, characters, and so forth. Students inquired about how the author got ideas for books, the actual day-to-day writing of the book, how the author edited the book, and even "How much money do you get?" Students were offered the opportunity to purchase a book of choice from the author's works and more than 100 of the 300 students who attended the author's talk purchased a book and had it autographed. This type of reading incentive takes careful planning, often beginning a year in advance. At many of our schools, the media specialists and reading specialists work together, often with the assistance of the Parent–Teacher Organization, to coordinate all aspects of the event. Memorable literacy experiences such as the author visit could not take place without thoughtful leadership and the efforts of a supportive literacy environment.

During my visit to this middle school, the English as a second language (ESL) teacher stopped at the reading specialist's office to ask for more picture books. The reading specialist and the ESL teacher had been teaming together to work with the English-language learners, reading high-level picture books to build reading skills and background knowledge. The students read the picture book once for decoding purposes and word knowledge, again for comprehension, and one final time to measure fluency. Students enjoyed these books so much that they, too, often stopped in the reading specialist's office to ask for additional books to take home for practice and to share with their family. This example illustrates the importance of providing appropriate materials and taking part in collaborative efforts so that reading specialists can assist in the literacy growth of all students.

When I visit any of the elementary or middle schools in our district, the reading specialist's office has a constant revolving door. As teachers, students, and administrators stop in to inquire about materials, discuss a recently read book, or ask for reading suggestions for themselves or struggling and advanced readers, the reading specialist has the opportunity to provide literacy leadership in a natural, collaborative setting. All of the literacy efforts mentioned throughout this book help raise students' interest in and enjoyment of reading, which help to raise reading performance. Our elementary and middle schools consistently have some of the highest state achievement scores in the area of English and reading and writing.

We end with a quote by MaryEllen Vogt, former president of the International Reading Association. On International Literacy Day in 2004, Vogt stated, "Expert teachers plus the right resources will create the quality education all countries hope to provide their children" ("IRA Celebrates," 2004, p. 3). Vogt emphasized the importance of using resources such as trained, highly qualified professionals. Expensive programs and materials, the latest computer fix—no resource is as beneficial as the input from a highly skilled reading specialist who works collaboratively with classroom teachers to develop all students' literacy potential and enthusiasm. It is our experience that the reading specialist, when serving as a school literacy leader—with the support of the administration, teachers, and parents—can be an incredible resource to all students' literacy growth.

APPENDIX A

Lessons for Active Thinking

LTHOUGH THE MIDDLE SCHOOL students with whom I work are familiar with testing, they often lack active thinking strategies that can help them become more efficient at testing and in completing in-class assignments. The following lessons, based on the PIRATES system developed by Hughes, Schumaker, Deshler, and Mercer (1987), are designed to help students realize that having a plan in place for taking a test is far more effective than random guessing. These lessons are effective in modeling strategies for students and teachers.

Active Thinking Strategies for Test-Taking

1. Mount a copy of Figure A.1 on colored paper and laminate. Give it to the teacher to display in the classroom so the strategies you are going to teach are reinforced.

2. Distribute a paper to each student with Figure A.2 on one side and Figure A.3 on the other. Use paper that has holes so that the notes can be inserted into the students' binders immediately following the lesson. Begin the lesson with a discussion about mnemonic devices. Ask if anyone knows what a mnemonic device is and then show Figure A.4. Allow the students to tell what the mnemonic devices are and ask if they have examples of others. Figure A.5 is notated and helps explain additional mnemonic devices that may be mentioned.

3. Ask the students to look at the side of the page that says, "What do I think PIRATES stands for?" (Figure A.2). Using students' knowledge of test taking, ask students to come up with ideas for what each letter might mean. After a few minutes, ask the students to share their ideas. This is an important step because the majority of the PIRATES

strategies will be mentioned and the remainder of the lesson will allow the students to organize them.

4. Once each letter has been discussed, have the students turn to the "PIRATES Test-Taking Strategies" page (Figure A.3). Present Figure A.6 on an overhead projector and uncover one letter at a time, allowing students time to fill in the notes. I have found that the framed notes are very effective because they keep the students on task and allow them to listen rather than try to copy every word. I had originally used framed notes only in the lower reading classes or with special education students, but found that they were more effective with everyone for this particular lesson. In addition, I use color to enhance my lesson. I write the strategies in one color and the details in another.

5. Figure A.7 should be presented in the investigation step and students can use the bottom of the page to plan their testing strategy. I explain that the order of the steps in the figure is what I find to be most effective but that students may choose to pursue the steps in a different order. The important point is that students need to have a plan in place.

6. For the estimating step, Figures A.8 and A.9 help provide a concrete example of each strategy: *eliminating similar choices* and *avoiding absolutes*. In the first question in Figure A.8, students should be able to eliminate immediately *chinchilla* as a choice because it is not a popular pet. Then, help students use the strategy of eliminating similar choices by pointing out that *cat* and *feline* are similar and can therefore be eliminated. In the second question in Figure A.8, ask students to identify similar choices and then eliminate the choices *one foot* and *thirteen inches*. After eliminating similar choices, students can reexamine the question and determine that the word *great* implies that the answer would be *three feet* not *eighteen inches* because three feet is greater.

For Figure A.9, ask students to determine whether the statement "All mammals give birth to live young" is true or false. Most students will believe the statement is true. However, a few students usually know that the platypus does not give birth to live young and share this information with the class. If no one knows this information, share it with the class. I usually show a picture to illustrate the fact. Have students revise the statement so it is true; for example, the statement could begin, "Most mammals..." or "Mammals usually...." Show students the list of absolute and safe words. Have students choose three absolute words and three safe words and create examples of each in their corresponding columns. Explain to students that absolutes can be true and ask students to brainstorm examples showing when an absolute is true (e.g., all triangles have three sides; the earth never stops rotating). By generating these examples, students learn to avoid using absolutes when they are unsure of an answer and use safe words instead because they are a better choice.

7. Once the notes have been completed, match students with a partner and have one partner ask as many questions about PIRATES as he or she can in one minute. The partners then switch roles and the other partner asks questions for another minute.

8. Finally, it is time to reverse roles. Students have their test-taking strategies in front of them while the teacher works through the practice test (Figure A.10). The teacher should think aloud about the strategies but make obvious mistakes that the students can catch if they are paying attention. Notated instructions appear in Figure A.11.

9. Depending on the attention span of the students and the length of the class period, you may wish to allow two class periods to complete this lesson.

Active Thinking Strategies for Reading Assignments and Assessments

1. Distribute a paper to each student with Figure A.2 on one side and Figure A.12 on the other. Use paper that has holes punched so that the notes can be inserted into the students' binders immediately following the lesson. Begin the lesson with a discussion about mnemonic devices. Ask if anyone knows what a mnemonic device is and then show Figure A.4 on an overhead projector. Allow the students to tell what the mnemonic devices are and then ask if they have examples of other mnemonic devices. Figure A.5 is notated and helps explain additional mnemonic devices that students may mention.

2. Ask the students to look at the side of the page that asks, "What do I think PIRATES stands for?" (Figure A.2). Using students' knowledge of test taking, ask students to come up with ideas for what each letter might mean. After a few minutes, ask the students to share their ideas. This is an important step because the majority of the PIRATES strategies will be mentioned and the remainder of the lesson will allow the students to organize them.

3. Once each letter has been discussed, have the students turn to the "PIRATES Active Thinking Strategies" page (Figure A.12). Present Figure A.13 on an overhead projector, uncovering one letter at a time and allowing students time to fill in the notes. I have found that the framed notes are very effective because they keep the students on task and allow them to listen rather than trying to copy every word. Originally I had used framed notes only in the lower reading classes or with special education students, but found that they were more effective with everyone for this particular lesson. In addition, I use color to enhance my lesson. I write the strategies in one color and the details in another.

4. After filling in the words ACTIVE READER in the investigate step, have students complete the Active Reading section at the bottom of the page.

5. For the estimating step, Figures A.8 and A.9 help provide a concrete example of each strategy: *eliminating similar choices* and *avoiding absolutes*. In the first question in Figure A.8, students should be able to immediately eliminate *chinchilla* as a choice because it is not a popular pet. Then, help students use the strategy of eliminating similar choices by pointing out to students that *cat* and *feline* are similar and can therefore be eliminated. In the second question in Figure A.8, ask students to identify similar choices and then eliminate the choices *one foot* and *thirteen inches*. After eliminating similar choices, students can reexamine the question and determine that the word *great* implies that the answer would be *three feet* not *eighteen inches* because three feet is greater.

For Figure A.9, ask students to determine whether the statement "All mammals give birth to live young" is true or false. Most students will believe the statement is true. However, a few students usually know that the platypus does not give birth to live young and share this information with the class. However, if no one knows this information, share it with the class. I usually show a picture to illustrate the fact. Have students revise the statement so it is true; for example, the statement could begin, "Most mammals..." or "Mammals usually...." Have students choose three absolute words and three safe words and create examples of each in their corresponding columns. Explain to students that absolutes can be true, and ask students to brainstorm examples showing when an absolute is true (e.g., all triangles have three sides; the earth never stops rotating). By generating these examples, students learn to avoid using absolutes when they are unsure of an answer and use safe words instead because they are a better choice.

6. Once the notes have been completed, match students with a partner and have one partner ask as many questions about PIRATES as he or she can in one minute. The partners then switch roles and the other partner asks questions for another minute.

7. Finally, it is time to reverse roles. Students have their test-taking strategies in front of them while the teacher works through a test. The teacher thinks aloud about the strategies but makes obvious mistakes that the students can catch if they are paying attention. Any short reading passage with appropriate questions can be used for demonstration. Such passages can be easily located in a grade-level literature book or reading resource book. Items from the test and notated instructions that appear in Figures A.10 and A.11 also could be used to reinforce the estimating strategies.

8. Depending on the attention span of the students and the length of the class period, you may wish to allow two class periods to complete this lesson.

FIGURE A.1
PIRATES TEST-TAKING STRATEGY

Prepare to succeed

Investigate

Read, remember, reduce

Answer or abandon

Turn back

Estimate

Survey

What do I think PIRATES stands for?

P

_____

I

_____

R

_____

A

_____

T

_____

E

_____

S

FIGURE A.3
PIRATES STUDENT NOTES

PIRATES Test-Taking Strategies

P_____ to _____
- Study
- _____
- Eat
- Write _____
- _____ over _____
- Think _____!

I_____
- Instructions: _____ them _____
- Underline _____
- Decide _____ to _____

R_____, remember, _____
- Read _____ question
- Read _____ answer _____
- _____ out _____ answers

A_____ or _____
- _____ the _____
  you _____

T _____ _____
- Return to _____ of _____
  or _____
- Answer _____ questions

E_____
- _____ the question
- Eliminate _____ answers
- Avoid _____
- Choose the _____ or
  most _____ answer

S_____
- Look over _____ test
- Make sure _____ answers are_____
- Don't _____ answers unless
  you are _____!

Test Order:
1. Read _____ questions
2. Do _____ the _____
3. Do true/_____ and _____ choice
4. Do _____ questions

Absolutes	"Safe" Words

FIGURE A.4
MNEMONIC WARM-UP

A rat in Tom's house may eat Tom's ice cream.

HOMES

My very elderly mother just served us nine pizzas.

FACE

Every good boy does fine.

Roy G. Biv

Please Excuse My Dear Aunt Sally

PIRATES

FIGURE A.5
MNEMONIC WARM-UP WITH NOTATIONS

A rat in Tom's house may eat Tom's ice cream.
(how to spell *arithmetic*)

HOMES
(five Great Lakes—Huron, Ontario, Michigan, Erie, and Superior)

My very elderly mother just served us nine pizzas.
(planets in order from the sun—Mercury, Venus, Earth, Mars, Jupiter, Saturn, Uranus, Neptune, and Pluto)

FACE
(music notes on the spaces of the treble staff)

Every good boy does fine.
(music notes on the lines of the treble staff—other variations include "Every good boy deserves fudge," "Elvis's guitar broke down Friday," and "Even George Bush drives fast")

Roy G. Biv
(color spectrum in order—red, orange, yellow, green, blue, indigo, and violet)

Please Excuse My Dear Aunt Sally
(order of math operations—parentheses, exponents, multiplication, division, addition, and subtraction)

PIRATES

FIGURE A.6
PIRATES TEST-TAKING STRATEGIES

Prepare to succeed	• Study • Sleep • Eat	• Write name • Look over test • Think positive
Investigate	• Instructions: Read them all • Underline specifics • Decide where to begin	
Read, remember, reduce	• Read whole question • Read all answer choices • Cross out wrong answers	
Answer or abandon	• Mark the questions you abandon	
Turn back	• Return to beginning of test or section • Answer abandoned questions	
Estimate	• Reexamine the question • Eliminate similar answers • Avoid absolutes • Choose the longest or most detailed answer	
Survey	• Look over entire test • Make sure all answers are completed • Don't change answers unless you are sure!	

Test Order:
1. Read essay questions
2. Do fill in the blanks
3. Do true/false and multiple choice
4. Do essay questions

Absolutes	"Safe" Words

FIGURE A.7
TEST ORDER

Where do I begin?

1. <u>Read</u> the essay questions.

2. <u>Do</u> fill-in-the-blank questions.

3. <u>Do</u> true/false and multiple-choice questions.

4. <u>Do</u> essay questions.

FIGURE A.8
ELIMINATING SIMILAR CHOICES

The most popular pet in the United States is a

a. cat

c. feline

b. dog

d. chinchilla

The average length of a great brown warlump is

a. one foot

c. three feet

b. thirteen inches

d. eighteen inches

FIGURE A.9
AVOIDING ABSOLUTES

True or False?

All mammals give birth to live young.

Absolutes	Safe Words
all	some
every	most
only	many
never	rarely
always	usually
none	few
exactly	approximately
	sometimes

Name: _____

Directions: Put the letter of the best answer in the blank next to the question.

____ Imbelic solution is
   a. used by scientists to break down compound materials for study
   b. radioactive

   c. a blue-gray color

   d. highly poisonous

____ The result of adding the preservative glucarate to lumber is as follows:
   a. it never rots
   b. it never changes color

   c. it always changes color
   d. it rarely rots

____ Architects stopped using exotriol in construction because
   a. it was not cost effective
   b. it was combustible

   c. it was not strong enough
   d. it was flammable

____ The northern gray snake primarily eats
   a. mice, moles, and shrews
   b. bird eggs

   c. nuts and berries
   d. small rodents

Directions: Put a T for True and an F for False on the line next to the question. Correct the statements that are false.

____ Every ciderberry tree produces fruit in the last week of June.
____ Most northern gray snakes grow to be approximately three feet long.
____ Northern gray snakes are tree dwellers and are rarely found on the ground.
____ Imbelic solution is the only solution used by scientists in researching the effects of glucarate on lumber.

Directions: Carefully read the sentence that explains what your topic is. Please print your essay.

Write a brief essay about the northern gray snake. Include specific information about its diet, habitat, and characteristics.

FIGURE A.11
PIRATES PRACTICE TEST WITH NOTATIONS

Jump into the test without looking over it. Students will immediately correct you, giving you the opportunity to demonstrate looking over the types of questions you have to answer, reviewing the instructions, and underlining important details. Read the essay question and ask students to be attentive to information about the topic.

Name: _____

Directions: Put the letter of the best answer in the blank next to the question.

_____ Imbelic solution is
    a. used by scientists to break down compound materials for study
    b. radioactive
    c. a blue-gray color
    d. highly poisonous

Eliminate similar answer choices—radioactive and highly poisonous *mean the same thing. Cross them out and go on to the next question. Students will usually remind you to mark the question because you abandoned it.*

_____ The result of adding the preservative glucarate to lumber is
    a. it never rots
    b. it never changes color
    c. it always changes color
    d. it rarely rots

Avoid absolutes—cross out choices a, b, and c.

_____ Architects stopped using exotriol in construction because
    a. it was not cost effective
    b. it was combustible
    c. it was not strong enough
    d. it was flammable

Eliminate similar answer choices—cross out choice b and d. Abandon question for further examination—remember to mark it or let students remind you. When you TURN BACK, ask the students to reexamine the question and think about what an architect does. The students generally come to the consensus that the architect designs the building and would be more concerned with strength than cost.

_____ The northern gray snake primarily eats
a. mice, moles, and shrews
c. nuts and berries
b. bird eggs
d. small rodents

Eliminate similar answer choices—a and d are the same thing. Allow student conversation, which will help students come to the conclusion that snakes do not eat berries or nuts and that choice c can be eliminated as well. Students usually will point out that this is the subject of the essay question.

Directions: Put a T for True and an F for False on the line next to the question. Correct the statements that are false.

Comment on how underlining instruction drew your eye back to the specific instructions so that you can complete this section correctly.

_____ Every ciderberry tree produces fruit in the last week of June.

Avoid absolutes—this statement can be corrected by replacing every *with* most *and rewriting the sentence to read "trees produce."*

_____ Most northern gray snakes grow to be approximately three feet long.

*Avoid absolutes—*approximately *is a safe word. We pay attention because this is this focus of the essay question.*

_____ Northern gray snakes are tree dwellers and are rarely found on the ground.

Students will point out readily that if you refer back to the question about the diet of the northern gray snake, this question makes sense.

_____ Imbelic solution is the only solution used by scientists in researching the effects of glucarate on lumber.

Avoid absolutes—students recognize the word only *as an absolute, which makes this question false, and will often mention that imbelic solution is mentioned in the first question. Reexamining the questions carefully confirms that a is the correct answer to the first question.*

Carefully read the sentence that explains what your topic is.
Please print your essay.

(continued)

Write a brief essay about the northern gray snake. Include specific information about its diet, habitat, and characteristics.

Ask the students what they could write about the northern gray snake. Have them share how they gathered information from the test questions. Turn back and answer questions that were abandoned.

PIRATES Test-Taking Strategies

P_____ to _____
- Study
- _____
- Eat
- Write _____
- _____ over _____
- Think _____!

I_____
- Instructions: _____ them _____
- Underline _____
- Read _____ before the _____
- Be an _____ _____!

R_____, remember, _____
- Read _____ question
- Read _____ answer _____
- _____ out _____ answers

A_____ or _____
- _____ the _____ you _____

T_____ _____
- Return to _____ of _____ or _____
- Answer _____ questions

E_____
- _____ the question
- Eliminate _____ answers
- Avoid _____
- Choose the _____ or most _____ answer

S_____
- Look over _____ test
- Make sure _____ answers are_____
- Don't _____ answers unless you are_____ !

Active Reading:
1._____
2._____
3._____
4._____

Absolutes	"Safe" Words

FIGURE A.13
PIRATES TEACHER NOTES FOR READING TESTS

PIRATES Test-Taking Strategies

Prepare to succeed	• Study • Sleep • Eat	• Write name • Look over test • Think positive!
Investigate	• Instructions: Read them all • Underline specifics • Read questions before the passage • Be an ACTIVE READER!	
Read, remember, reduce	• Read whole question • Read all answer choices • Cross out wrong answers	
Answer or abandon	• Mark the questions you abandon	
Turn back	• Return to beginning of test or section • Answer abandoned questions	
Estimate	• Reexamine the question • Eliminate similar answers • Avoid absolutes • Choose the longest or most detailed answer	
Survey	• Look over entire test • Make sure all answers are completed • Don't change answers unless you are sure!	

Active Reading:	Absolutes	"Safe" Words
1. Set purpose 2. Underline/highlight 3. Take notes 4. Reread		

Leading a Successful Reading Program: Administrators and Reading Specialists Working Together to Make It Happen by Nancy DeVries Guth and Stephanie Stephens Pettengill. Copyright © 2005 International Reading Association. May be copied for classroom use.

Lessons for Active Reading

ORIGINALLY BEGAN DEVELOPING the following series of lessons so that I could have the opportunity to present reading strategies to all sixth-grade students. I quickly found that the lessons served another purpose, that of staff development. The lessons provide teachers with strategies that they can use in the classroom to reinforce active reading. Prior to beginning the lessons, meet with the teacher to find out which content area book the students will have available for reference and which chapter they are currently studying. Ask if there are concepts that the students are having particular difficulty with so that you can review and reinforce the information through your lessons.

Before Reading: Lesson 1

1. Distribute Figure B.1 to the students and display it on an overhead projector. Ask students to think about what they do to help them remember what they read. Have them write down their ideas in the first section and then share their ideas with a partner. Students should write down in the second section of the page any new ideas they hear during this exchange. After a few minutes, ask students to share some of the ideas with the class. At this point, you should mention some of the strategies that will be covered in the lesson; this will help generate background knowledge for the lesson. Explain that this paper will be collected and returned to students in two weeks. When it is returned, students will be asked to list some new strategies in the third section of the page. Ask students to make sure their names are on the paper and then collect papers and label them with identifying information, such as name and class.

2. Display Figure B.2 and explain to the students that comprehension is the goal of reading and that comprehension only occurs through ac-

tive reading. Point out that good readers are active before, during, and after reading and emphasize the characteristics that are found at each stage.

3. Present Figure B.3 in order to prove that certain criteria must be in place before comprehension can occur and to hook students into the lesson. Give students a minute to read the paragraph silently (or it can be read aloud) and then ask them to identify what the passage is about. After students have generated a few ideas, examine the passage: Were the words too difficult? Are the sentences incomplete? Why can't we understand what the author is saying? Place Figure B.4 over the passage and ask students to read it again. After a few sentences a chorus of "Oh, now I get it!" will begin, and the students will begin to realize that what occurs before reading is truly important to comprehension.

4. Distribute Figure B.5 to each student.

5. Display Figure B.6 and share the thoughts of the active reader with the class.

6. Place Figure B.7 on the overhead projector and ask students to read aloud the introductory statement and underline keywords. Explain the three-column note format that they will be using and that the third column can be used to list examples or create illustrations.

7. Begin filling in the notes on the overhead, uncovering one strategy at a time.

8. Demonstrate "Judge a book by its cover" by showing two or three books that have covers that tell a lot about the story. I have used *Island: Shipwreck* (Korman, 1992), which clearly shows six present-day adolescents stranded on an island in the ocean, and *Lyddie* (Paterson, 1992), which shows a young girl dressed in old-fashioned clothing working in some type of factory. The students are often surprised at how much background information they can formulate from the cover of the book.

9. Explain that reading the summary can help you identify if the book is too difficult to be read independently. To determine this, I draw a hand, number the fingers, and share the method of reading the summary or a random paragraph from the text and count the number of words that the students cannot identify. If they find five words right away (not counting proper names), the book may be too difficult to read independently.

10. Ask the students to take out their social studies or science texts and use the current chapter of study to demonstrate previewing pictures and captions and reading charts, graphs, and maps.

11. Display the table of contents from another book to demonstrate how using a table of contents can serve as a preview and review and can assist in making predictions. (The content area book can also be used for this purpose.)

12. Explain how formulating questions can be used to monitor comprehension of previously read material before continuing with the text. Demonstrate how to think aloud using a novel the students are familiar with such as *Holes* (Sachar, 1998). For example, I might demonstrate the strategy by stating,

> I'm ready to start chapter 5, so let me think.... Who? Stanley Yelnats is the main character. Mr. Sir works at the camp he was sent to. What is happening? Stanley has been arrested for stealing shoes and is being sent to a detention camp. When? The story takes place in the present. Where? Camp Green Lake in Texas. Why? Stanley thinks it is all because of a family curse. How? Stanley ended up there because no one believed that he had actually found the shoes.

At this point, I ask students if they think I have comprehended what is happening and should begin reading chapter 5. Then, I model how this strategy can help me realize that I need to review with the following think aloud.

> Who? I think the main character was a kid. I'm pretty sure it was a boy. What is happening? He's on a bus going somewhere. I think he might be going camping. When? I'm not sure yet. Where? I know that wherever he is going, it is hot.

Finally, I stop and ask the students if they think I am ready to continue reading the book. I explain that if they cannot remember who the story is about, what is happening, and when and where the story takes place, most likely they are not comprehending and need to reread or review.

13. Refer to the text to examine how new words are introduced: Are they in bold print? Are they highlighted? Are new vocabulary words introduced at the beginning of the chapter? Carefully examining and attempting to pronounce these words in advance will assist with fluency and comprehension.

14. Remind students that simply talking about what has been read with another student is an effective strategy. Discussing a novel or an assigned reading with a friend can confirm comprehension or alert the reader that review is necessary.

15. Ask the students to help you fill in the *K* and *W* columns of the K-W-L chart using a concept that you have previously decided upon with the classroom teacher. Figure B.8 is a blank K-W-L chart and Figure B.9 shows an example of a K-W-L chart that was generated during one of my lessons.

16. Remind the students that they are already familiar with a Think–Pair–Share—it was the activity the lesson began with. I also tell students that this strategy can even be done over the telephone—a definite plus for adolescents.

17. Emphasize the fact that a summary is short, does not contain a lot of details, and that if the previously read material cannot be summarized in a few sentences, a review is probably necessary.

18. Ask students to refer to their binders to examine materials such as notes, study guides, returned assignments, or graphic organizers. Discuss how reviewing these materials prior to reading or rereading a section or chapter of the text can improve comprehension.

19. Refer to the content area textbook and examine the questions at the end of the chapter. Discuss the different types of questions: Which questions will have an answer that is found directly in the text? Which questions will require you to use information that you already know in conjunction with the material in the textbook? This serves as a good segue to a future lesson on Question–Answer Relationship (QAR), a system of examining questions (Raphael, 1986) that is used widely and with great success at the elementary and middle school levels.

20. Conclude the lesson by referring again to Figure B.6 and asking the students to keep those thoughts in mind as they try the strategies throughout the week. Remind students that next week they will be asked to share strategies that they tried.

21. Ask students to place the strategies in their binder for easy reference.

During Reading: Lesson 2

1. Review Figure B.2.

2. Ask students to refer to their notes from the previous lesson. Display Figure B.7 to assist any students who do not have their notes.

3. Allow students time to share the strategies that they used and whether or not they found them effective.

4. Distribute Figure B.10 to the students.

5. Display Figure B.11. Share and discuss the thoughts of the active reader, stressing the fact that **reading must make sense**.

6. Display Figure B.12. Ask the students to read aloud the introductory statement and underline keywords. Review the three-column note format.

7. Begin filling in the notes on the overhead, uncovering one strategy at a time.

8. Discuss the meaning of the word *clarify* with the students. Explain that sometimes we have difficulty understanding the **meaning** of the text or of the word and sometimes we have difficulty recognizing the **word**.

9. Illustrate how to use context clues to clarify meaning by showing an example of how the text surrounding a word can help with comprehension. I use the example of a student who came to me and said, "My teacher told me I'm belligerent. What does that mean?" I ask the students to raise their hands if they think belligerent is a good thing and then ask them to raise their hands if they think it is a bad thing. Most of the students usually are not sure. I uncover the word in Figure B.13 and ask the students if they recognize it and if looking at the word helps them understand it. I then uncover the sentence, read it aloud, and again ask for a show of hands as to whether belligerent is a positive or negative behavior. Then I ask students to tell what context clues helped them to recognize the meaning of the word.

10. Illustrate how context clues can help readers identify a word that is in their listening and speaking vocabularies by using the next two examples in Figure B.13. The two words I share with students are words that they miss often when I give a reading test. They are words that students are familiar with, but they cannot be sounded

out phonetically and are not seen in print very often. Emphasize to the students that they have to be absolutely silent and not read aloud the word. Uncover the word *cushion*. Ask for a show of hands to see who thinks they know the word and who is not sure. Uncover the sentence with the word in context and have the class read it aloud. Follow the same procedure with the word *yacht*.

11. Demonstrate how chunking a word can make it easier to pronounce by using the examples in Figure B.14. Examine how prefixes, suffixes, and roots have meaning attached that can help you define a word.

12. Use Figure B.15 to show how an active reader uses the K-W-L chart while reading.

13. Use the examples in Figure B.16 to show how mapping can be used to take notes while reading and to organize information. Write the current unit of study in the center and allow the students to come up with other examples to go in the detail circles surrounding the center circle.

14. Provide the students with Figures B.17 and B.18 to show examples of what two- and three-column notes might look like. Students should be instructed to take notes in their own words and to use the third column to illustrate or elaborate on the concepts.

15. Display the story map in Figure B.19 and allow the students to guide you in filling it out using a novel they have read in class. I explain to students that the story map is an active map for active readers. Do not complete one box at a time, but rather continually add information about setting, characters, and events as they appear in the text.

16. Use a chapter from a social studies or science text to demonstrate how the authors give readers the information in short sections. I demonstrate this for students by reading a section, doing a think-aloud summary, reading the next section, and then doing a think-aloud summary in which I realize that I did not understand what I read. I ask the students if I have to go all the way back to the beginning of the passage to begin rereading. In most cases, students point out that I was able to summarize the first section, so I do not have to go back so far; but, if they do not point this out, I demonstrate it for them.

17. Emphasize how important discussion is to comprehension. (I make it a point to model this constantly.) Before I begin any lesson, I generate a discussion about the novel that is currently being read in class, the novels on the Virginia Young Readers list, the books that I see on the students' desks—anything to generate conversation about literature.

18. Remind students to put the notes in their binders so that they can refer to them and use them during the final lesson. Encourage them to try the strategies during the week so that they can share their successes.

After Reading: Lesson 3

1. Review Figure B.2.

2. Ask students to refer to their notes from the previous lessons.

3. Allow students time to share the strategies that they used during the past week and whether or not they found them effective.

4. Distribute Figure B.20 to the students.

5. Explain to students that they now have so many strategies that they are active readers and can now draw their faces on the figure. Give them a few minutes to work on their self-portraits.

6. Display Figure B.21 on the overhead projector. Uncover the thought bubbles one at a time and discuss the specifics of each strategy.

7. Return the Think–Pair–Share (Figure B.1) that was done at the beginning of the first lesson to each student.

8. Give students two or three minutes to write down all of the comprehension strategies they can recall—without using their notes. Give them an additional two or three minutes to then use their notes to write down additional strategies. This can be a very empowering activity for students because most of them will have very little written in the first two sections. Being able to fill the entire bottom page and often part of the back page provides students with a great visual of how much they have learned. Figure B.22 and B.23 show examples of student work.

9. Divide the class into four or five teams for Active Reading Jeopardy, which helps to reinforce all of the strategies you have taught. Designate two score keepers or ask the teacher to keep score.

Present the game board in Figure B.24 and go over the categories. Team A chooses a category and amount. If they answer the question correctly, then it is Team B's turn. Team B chooses a category and amount. If they answer the question incorrectly, then Team C gets a chance to answer it. If Team C answers the question correctly, they are awarded the points and it becomes Team D's turn. (I have learned that if a team "steals" a question and then gets another turn, the scores get too far apart for the game to be competitive.)

10. Let the game begin. Read the questions from Figure B.25 as they are selected. You can allow the students to use their notes and confer with their teams before answering, if desired.

11. Reward all students with a bookmark, candy, or pencil and then reward the winning team with an additional treat. While some educators argue that students do not need extrinsic rewards, I find as a reading specialist that it is a good public relations tool to use with the students.

12. Finally, collect and comment on the Think–Pair–Share activity. I take some time to skim the students' papers and write a brief comment on each one before returning them. This only takes a few minutes and, again, sends the message that they have been successful and that I value them as members of the school literacy community.

Think! How do you help yourself remember what you read?

Pair... Share! What ideas do others have?

Great ideas! Here are the things I learned to do to increase comprehension!

Before Reading

ACTIVATE PRIOR KNOWLEDGE

SET PURPOSE

During Reading

SELF MONITOR

CONNECTIONS

MAKE

After Reading

SUMMARIZE

REACT

PREDICT

EXTEND

A seashore is a better place than a street. At first it is better to run than walk. Also, you may have to try several times. It takes some skill but it's easy to learn. Even young children can enjoy it. Birds seldom get too close. Rain soaks in very fast. If there are no complications it can be very peaceful.

Adapted from *Project CRISS training manual.* (1996). Dubuque, IA: Kendall/Hunt.

FIGURE B.4
KITE OVERLAY FOR READING PASSAGE

FIGURE B.5
BEFORE READING STUDENT NOTES

Name:_____

BEFORE reading I activate my BACKGROUND KNOWLEDGE and SET A PURPOSE.

Strategies/activities to use BEFORE reading:

Predict	• Think about what might _____ based on what you _____	
Judge a book by its cover	• Look for information about the _____, _____, and _____ in the _____ and _____	
Read summary	• Gives you a _____ for reading • Helps you know if the _____ is too _____ to read by _____	
Preview pictures and captions	• _____ pictures _____ • Helps you _____ while you are _____	
Read charts, graphs, and maps	• Look for _____ and _____ information in the _____ of the book	
Read/review table of contents	• Chapter titles _____ your memory and help you _____	
Formulate questions	Who? _____? When? _____? Why? _____?	

(continued)

Scan for high-lighted or unfamiliar words	• Try to _____out keywords _____ you read so you won't have to_____	
Discuss with peer, teacher, or parent	• _____ about what you _____ helps you remember it	
Create K-W-L chart	• What I _____ • What I _____ to know • What I _____	
Think–Pair–Share	• _____or _____ what you know about a _____ • Get with a _____ and _____	
Summarize previously read material	• Think about what you _____ read • A _____ is _____ • If you can't _____what you read, _____ before you go to on	
Review notes or graphic organizers	• Look at _____, Venn diagram, _____, story map, _____. for review	
Read questions at the end of the chapter or passage	• Sometimes there are _____ at the _____ of the chapter • Gives you _____ to _____ for while you read	

FIGURE B.7
BEFORE READING TEACHER NOTES

Name:_____

BEFORE reading I activate my BACKGROUND KNOWLEDGE and SET A PURPOSE.

Strategies/activities to use BEFORE reading:

Predict	• Think about what might ___happen___ based on what you ___know___	
Judge a book by its cover	• Look for information about the ___plot___, ___characters___, and ___setting___ in the ___title___ and ___illustrations___	
Read summary	• Gives you a ___purpose___ for reading • Helps you know if the ___book___ is too ___difficult___ to read by ___yourself___	
Preview pictures and captions	• ___Examine___ pictures ___carefully___ • Helps you ___visualize___ while you are ___reading___	
Read charts, graphs, and maps	• Look for ___author notes___ and ___historical___ information in the ___back___ of the book	
Read/review table of contents	• Chapter titles ___refresh___ your memory and help you ___predict___	
Formulate questions	Who? ___What___? When? ___Where___? Why? ___How___?	

(continued)

Scan for high-lighted or unfamiliar words	• Try to _figure_ out keywords _before_ you read so you won't have to _stop_	
Discuss with peer, teacher, or parent	• _Talking_ about what you _read_ helps you remember it	
Create K-W-L chart	• What I _Know_ • What I _Want_ to know • What I _Learned_	K | W | L
Think–Pair–Share	• _Think_ or _write_ what you know about a _topic_ • Get with a _partner_ and _share_	
Summarize previously read material	• Think about what you _already_ read • A _summary_ is _short_ • If you can't _remember_ what you read, _review_ before you go to on	
Review notes or graphic organizers	• Look at _notes_, Venn diagram, _KWL_, story map, _etc_. for review	
Read questions at the end of the chapter or passage	• Sometimes there are _questions_ at the _end_ of the chapter • Gives you _something_ to _look_ for while you read	

FIGURE B.8
K-W-L CHART

Topic: _____

What I **K**now	What I **W**ant to know	What I **L**earned

From Ogle, D.M. (1986). K-W-L: A teaching model that develops active reading of expository text. *The Reading Teacher, 39,* 564–570.

Topic: __WWI__

What I **K**now	What I **W**ant to know	What I **L**earned
The United States was involved. Many countries in Europe were involved. The war was not fought in the United States. The war took place before the 1920s. Grover Cleveland was the president of the United States.	Why did the war begin? Why did the United States get involved? Which countries were involved? Where did the fighting occur? Did most people in the United States agree with or oppose the war? In what years was the war fought? What was the outcome?	

From Ogle, D.M. (1986). K-W-L: A teaching model that develops active reading of expository text. *The Reading Teacher, 39,* 564–570.

FIGURE B.10
DURING READING STUDENT NOTES

Name: _____

DURING reading I SELF-MONITOR and MAKE CONNECTIONS.

Strategies/activities to use DURING reading:

Self-monitoring	• Is this making _____? • If it doesn't make sense, _____ and _____ it!	
Clarify meaning	• Reread • Use _____ clues • Take _____ • Ask for _____ • Illustrate • _____ it up	
Clarify words	• Phonics - _____ it _____ • Context clues • Look for word _____ - _____	
K-W-L	• _____ information in the *K* column • Get _____ for the *W* column • _____ in the *L* column	
Mapping	• _____ in information as you _____	
Two- or three-column notes	• Help _____ information • Set them up in _____ way _____ for you	
Story map	• Helps _____ and summarize • Can be used for any _____	
Section, stop, and summarize	• Break reading into _____ • _____ and think about what _____	

FIGURE B.12
DURING READING TEACHER NOTES

Name: _____

DURING reading I SELF-MONITOR and MAKE CONNECTIONS.

Strategies/activities to use DURING reading:

Self-monitoring	• Is this making _____sense_____ ? • If it doesn't make sense, _____stop_____ and _____fix_____ it!	
Clarify meaning	• Reread • Use _____context_____ clues • Take _____notes_____ • Ask for _____help_____ • Illustrate • _____Look_____ it up	
Clarify words	• Phonics— _____sound_____ it _____out_____ • Context clues • Look for word _____parts_____ — _____"chunks"_____	
K-W-L	• _____Correct_____ information in the _K_ column • Get _____answers_____ for the _W_ column • _____Fill_____ in the _L_ column	
Mapping	• _____Fill_____ in information as you _____read_____	
Two- or three-column notes	• Help _____organize_____ information • Set them up in _____whatever_____ way _____works_____ for you	
Story map	• Helps _____organize_____ and summarize • Can be used for any _____subject_____	
Section, stop, and summarize	• Break reading into _____sections_____ • _____Stop_____ and think about what _____happened_____	

FIGURE B.13
USING CONTEXT CLUES

belligerent

The boy was called to the principal's office for being belligerent. He ignored the teacher, slammed his books down, and refused to do his work.

cushion

Put the cushion back on the couch.

yacht

The magnificent yacht sailed across the ocean taking its passengers on a relaxing vacation getaway.

Leading a Successful Reading Program: Administrators and Reading Specialists Working Together to Make It Happen by Nancy DeVries Guth and Stephanie Stephens Pettengill. Copyright © 2005 International Reading Association. May be copied for classroom use.

FIGURE B.14
CHUNKING WORDS TO FIND PRONUNCIATION AND MEANING

Chunking words can help with pronounciation...

reconstruction   = re con struc tion

misinterpreted   = mis in ter pret ed

...and meaning!

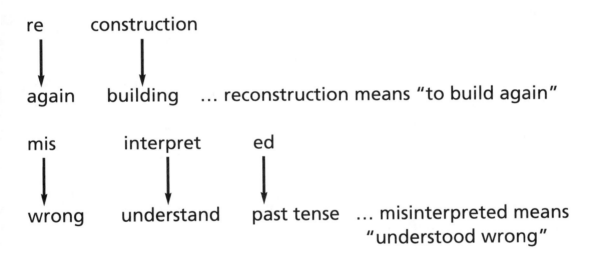

re   construction

again   building ... reconstruction means "to build again"

mis   interpret   ed

wrong   understand   past tense ... misinterpreted means "understood wrong"

Which doctor would I see for a heart problem?

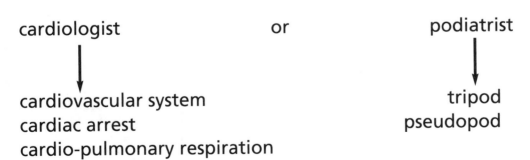

cardiologist   or   podiatrist

cardiovascular system   tripod
cardiac arrest   pseudopod
cardio-pulmonary respiration

FIGURE B.15
COMPLETED K-W-L CHART FOR DURING READING LESSON

Topic: WWI

What I **K**now	What I **W**ant to know	What I **L**earned
The United States was involved. Many countries in Europe were involved. The war was not fought in the United States. The war took place before the 1920s. Grover Cleveland was the president of the United States.	Why did the war begin? Why did the United States get involved? Which countries were involved? Where did the fighting occur? Did most people in the United States agree with or oppose the war? In what years was the war fought? What was the outcome?	Conflicts among countries in Europe, militarism, forming of secret alliances, assassination of Archduke Ferdinand and Duchess Sophie. Five merchant ships were sunk by Germany after they had promised to leave passenger ships alone.

Allied Powers	Central Powers
Serbia Britain France Russia Belgium Italy United States	Austria-Hungary Germany Bulgaria Ottoman Empire

From Ogle, D.M. (1986). K-W-L: A teaching model that develops active reading of expository text. *The Reading Teacher, 39,* 564–570.

FIGURE B.16
MAPPING DURING READING

Mapping
- Helps organize information
- Requires you to be an active reader
- Can be used as a study guide

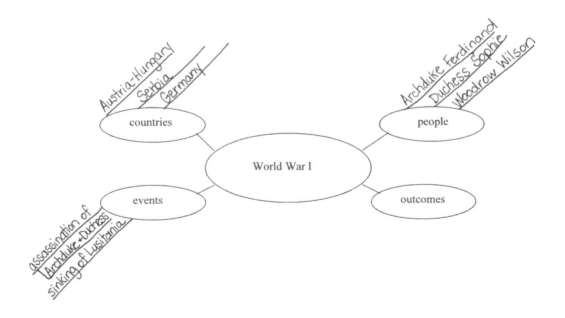

FIGURE B.17
TWO-COLUMN NOTES

Two-Column Notes

- help you organize information
- require you to be an active reader
- are written in your own words
- can be used as a study guide
- can be used for any subject

****

Science...	Matter
Solids	have a definite shape take up space have weight
Liquids	take the shape of their container take up space have weight

****

Social Studies...	Westward Expansion
Miners	came because of new discoveries of gold and silver camps grew into towns—businesses and farms were started refineries were built problems arose because of lack of law enforcement boomtowns became ghost towns when resources ran out

(continued)

Ranchers	lots of cattle ranches in Texas in early 1800s
	cities in the east grew after the Civil War
	more people = need for more food
	slow and expensive to get cattle to the East by water
	started taking cattle on long drives to the railroad
	cattle got to the cities faster and cheaper

****

Language Arts/ Reading...	*The Graduation of Jake Moon*
Alzheimer's	a disease that causes memory loss and confusion; it gets worse over time and is found in old people
pathetic	sad; pitiful; a person or thing you would feel sorry for

FIGURE B.18
THREE-COLUMN NOTES

Three-Column Notes

- help you organize information
- require you to be an active reader
- are written in your own words

- can be used as a study guide
- can be used for any subject
- allow you to add more details or illustrations

****

Science...	Matter	
Solids	have a definite shape take up space have weight	chair, desk, rock, tree
Liquids	take the shape of their container take up space have weight	water, juice, milk

****

Social Studies...	Westward Expansion	
Miners	came because of new discoveries of gold and silver camps grew into towns—businesses and farms were started refineries were built problems arose because of lack of law enforcement boomtowns became ghost towns when resources ran out	

(continued)

| Ranchers | lots of cattle ranches in Texas in early 1800s
cities in the east grew after the Civil War
more people = need for more food
slow and expensive to get cattle to the east by water
started taking cattle on long drives to the railroad
cattle got to the cities faster and cheaper |  |

****

Language Arts/ Reading...	*The Graduation of Jake Moon*	
Alzheimer's	a disease that causes memory loss and confusion; it gets worse over time and is found in old people	Jake's grandfather forgets things because he has Alzheimer's.
pathetic	sad; pitiful; a person or thing you would feel sorry for	It was pathetic to see such a smart man forget simple things.

FIGURE B.19
STORY MAP

Title/Author:	Setting (place/time period):

Characters:

Problem:

Important Events:

Outcome (must connect to the problem):

Think! How do you help yourself remember what you read?

I read out loud to myself, and I remember a lot.

Pair... Share! What ideas do others have?

Shanice-writes a summary of the first few chapters

Lauren-compares stories

Jake-stores it in his memory

Great ideas! Here are the things I learned to do to increase comprehension!

- KWL chart
- think pair, share
- predict
- summarize
- react
- extend
- recall and retell
- SQ3R
- graphs
- pictures

- take notes
- memorize
- write a paper
- go over
- picture in your mind
- draw
- ask for help

FIGURE B.23
COMPLETED THINK–PAIR–SHARE

Think! How do you help yourself remember what you read?

Read the page again.

Pair... Share! What ideas do others have?

Think how the character got in the situation in the first place.

Great ideas! Here are the things I learned to do to increase comprehension!

- KWL
- Story Map
- Two or Three column notes
- Sound-it-out
- VENN Diagram
- RE-Read
- Judge book by cover
- predict
- Summarize
- self-Monitoring

- Think-pair-share
- Look over pictures
- read charts and graphs
- read table of contents
- formulate questions
- Scan for Highlights words
- Discuss with peer
- Mapping

Leading a Successful Reading Program: Administrators and Reading Specialists Working Together to Make It Happen by Nancy DeVries Guth and Stephanie Stephens Pettengill. Copyright © 2005 International Reading Association. May be copied for classroom use.

FIGURE B.24
ACTIVE READERS JEOPARDY BOARD

Before Reading	During Reading	After Reading	Anything Goes
100	100	100	100
200	200	200	200
300	300	300	300
400	400	400	400
500	500	500	500

FIGURE B.25
READING JEOPARDY QUESTIONS

Before Reading	During Reading	After Reading	Anything Goes
Doing this can help you find out if the book is too difficult. (read the summary)	These notes are easy to use and help keep you organized. (two- and three-column notes)	When you do this, you decide how you felt about what you read. (react)	The goal of reading is.... * (comprehension)
This strategy helps you get information about the characters, setting, and plot. (judging a book by its cover)	If you don't understand something, what should you go back and do? (reread)	This happens when you think about what you just read. (summarize)	This type of reader comprehends. * (active)
If chapter titles are available this can help you review and refresh your memory. (reading the table of contents)	This graphic organizer is effective for helping you keep track of what is happening in a novel. * (story map)	This graphic organizer is effective for nonfiction and is used before, during, and after reading. (K-W-L)	What could you look for at the end of the chapter to help set a purpose for reading? (questions)
Name the two main things that active readers do before reading. (set a purpose and activate background knowledge)	Name the two main things that active readers do during reading. * (make connections and self-monitor)	Name four things that active readers do after reading. (predict, react, summarize, and extend)	Name three strategies you could use to identify an unfamiliar word. * (sound it out, chunk it, use context clues, look it up)
Doing this will help you visualize as you read a new chapter in a textbook. * (preview the pictures and captions)	When you ask yourself if the text is making sense, you are doing this. (self-monitoring)	Looking for more information about a particular subject would be an example of this. (extending your knowledge)	Name two strategies that are used before, during, and after reading. * (K-W-L, predict, summarize)

* Denotes questions I used as "daily doubles."

References

Allington, R.L. (1998). The schools we have. The schools we need. In C. Weaver (Ed.), *Reconsidering a balanced approach to reading* (pp. 495–519). Urbana, IL: National Council of Teachers of English.

Allington, R.L. (2001). *What really matters for struggling readers.* New York: Longman.

Allington, R.L. (2002). Research on reading/learning disability interventions. In A.E. Farstrup & S.J. Samuels (Eds.), *What research has to say about reading instruction* (3rd ed., pp. 261–290). Newark, DE: International Reading Association.

Allington, R.L., & Cunningham, P.M. (2002). *Schools that work: Where all children read and write* (2nd ed.). New York: Longman.

Au, K.H. (1993). *Literacy instruction in multicultural settings.* Fort Worth, TX: Harcourt Brace.

Bean, R.M. (2002). Developing an effective reading program. In S.B. Wepner, D.S. Strickland, & J.T. Feeley (Eds.), *The administration and supervision of reading programs* (3rd ed., pp. 3–15). New York: Teachers College Press.

Bean, R.M. (2004). *The reading specialist: Leadership for the classroom, school, and community.* New York: Guilford.

Beers, K. (1998). Choosing not to read: Understanding why some middle schoolers just say no. In K. Beers & B. Samuels (Eds.), *Into focus: Understanding and creating middle school readers* (pp. 37–63). Norwood, MA: Christopher-Gordon.

Beers, K. (2003). *When kids can't read, what teachers can do: A guide for teachers, 6–12.* Portsmouth, NH: Heinemann.

Cazden, C.B. (1979). Learning to read in classroom interaction. In L.B. Resnick & P.A. Weaver (Eds.), *Theory and practice of early reading* (Vol. 3, pp. 295–306). Hillsdale, NJ: Erlbaum.

Coaches, controversy, consensus. (2004, April/May). *Reading Today, 21*(5), pp. 1, 7.

Cunningham, P.M., & Allington, R.L. (1999). *Classrooms that work: They can all read and write* (2nd ed). New York: Longman.

Darling-Hammond, L. (1994). Performance-based assessment and educational equity. *Harvard Educational Review, 64*(1), 5–30.

Dewey, J. (1966). *Democracy in education: An introduction to the philosophy of education.* New York: Free Press. (Original work published 1916)

Dole, J.A. (2004). The changing role of the reading specialist in school reform. *The Reading Teacher, 57,* 462–471.

Gambrell, L.B., Dromsky, A.J., & Mazzoni, A.A. (2000). Motivation matters, fostering full access to literacy. In K.D. Wood & T.S. Dickinson (Eds.), *Promoting literacy in grades 4–9: A handbook for teachers and administrators* (pp. 128–138). Boston: Allyn & Bacon.

Grisham, D.L., Lapp, D., & Flood, J. (2000). The role of the teacher in the literacy program. In K.D. Wood & T.S. Dickinson (Eds.), *Promoting literacy in grades 4–9: A handbook for teachers and administrators* (pp. 17–39). Boston: Allyn & Bacon.

Guth, N.D. (2002). Community literacy day: A new school develops community support. *The Reading Teacher, 56,* 234–236.

Hughes, C.A., Schumaker, J.B., Deshler, D.D., & Mercer, C.D. (1993). *The test-taking strategy* (4th ed.). Lawrence, KS: Edge Enterprises.

International Reading Association. (2000). *Teaching all children to read: The roles of the reading specialist.* A position statement of the International Reading Association. Newark, DE: Author.

International Reading Association. (2003). *Investment in teacher preparation in the United States*. A position statement of the International Reading Association. Newark, DE: Author.

IRA Celebrates International Literacy Day at the Library of Congress. (2004, October/November). *Reading Today, 22*(3), p. 3.

Irvin, J.L., & Strauss, S.E. (2000). Developmental tasks of early adolescence: The foundation of an effective literacy learning program. In K.D. Wood & T.S. Dickinson (Eds.), *Promoting literacy in grades 4–9: A handbook for teachers and administrators* (pp. 115–127). Boston: Allyn & Bacon.

Kasten, W.C., & Wilfong, L.G. (2005). Encouraging independent reading with ambience: The book bistro in middle and secondary school classes. *Journal of Adolescent & Adult Literacy, 48*, 656–664.

Krashen, S.D. (2004). *The power of reading: Insights from the research* (2nd ed.). Portsmouth, NH: Heinemann.

Lipson, M.Y., Mosenthal, J.H., Mekkelsen, J., & Russ, B. (2004). Building knowledge and fashioning success one school at a time. *The Reading Teacher, 57*, 534–542.

Lowery-Moore, H. (1998). Voices of middle school readers. In K. Beers & B. Samuels (Eds.), *Into focus: Understanding and creating middle school readers* (pp. 23–35). Norwood, MA: Christopher-Gordon.

Mathewson, G.C. (1994). Model of attitude influence upon reading and learning to read. In R.B. Ruddell, M.R. Ruddell, & H. Singer (Eds.), *Theoretical models and processes of reading* (4th ed., pp. 1131–1160). Newark, DE: International Reading Association.

Mehan, H. (1979). *Learning lessons: Social organization in the classroom*. Cambridge, MA: Harvard University Press.

Moore, D. (2000). Settings for school literacy programs. In K.D. Wood & T.S. Dickinson (Eds.), *Promoting literacy in grades 4–9: A handbook for teachers and administrators* (pp. 53–62). Boston: Allyn & Bacon.

Mueller, P.N. (2001). *Lifers: Learning from at-risk adolescent readers*. Portsmouth, NH: Heinemann.

Ogle, D.M. (1986). K-W-L: A teaching model that develops active reading of expository text. *The Reading Teacher, 39*, 564–570.

Ogle, D.M. (2002). *Coming together as readers*. Arlington Heights, IL: Pearson.

Oldfather, P. (1995). Commentary: What's needed to maintain and extend motivation for literacy in the middle grades. *Journal of Reading, 38*(6), 420–422.

O'Neal, S. & Kapinus, B. (2000). Standards in the middle, moving beyond the basics. In K. D. Wood & T.S. Dickinson (Eds.), *Promoting literacy in grades 4–9: A handbook for teachers and administrators* (pp. 97–112). Boston: Allyn & Bacon.

Pearson, P.D. (2000). Foreword. In L. Robb, *Teaching reading in middle school* (pp. 6–7). New York: Scholastic Professional Books.

Powell-Brown, A. (2004). Can you be a teacher of literacy if you don't love to read? *Journal of Adolescent & Adult Literacy, 47*, 284–288.

Project CRISS training manual. (1996). Dubuque, IA: Kendall/Hunt.

Raphael, T.E. (1986). Teaching question answer relationships, revisited. *The Reading Teacher, 39*, 516–522.

Rasinski, T., & Padak, N. (2000). *Effective reading strategies: Teaching children who find reading difficult* (2nd ed.). New York: Prentice Hall.

Schiefele, U. (1991). Interest, learning and motivation. *Educational Psychologist, 26*, 299–323.

Smith, F. (1997). *Reading without nonsense* (3rd ed.). New York: Teachers College Press.

Spotlight on Reading Coaches. (2004, June/July). *Reading Today, 21*(6), pp. 1, 3.

Stanovich, K.E. (1986). Matthew effects in reading: Some consequences of individual differences in the acquisition of literacy. *Reading Research Quarterly, 21*, 360–407.

Strickland, D.S., Ganske, K., & Monroe, J.K. (2002). *Supporting struggling readers and writers; Strategies for classroom intervention 3–6.* Portland, ME: Stenhouse; Newark, DE: International Reading Association.

Tatum, A.W. (2004). A road map for reading specialists entering schools without exemplary reading programs: Seven quick lessons. *The Reading Teacher, 58,* 28–39.

Tompkins, G.E. (2001). *Literacy for the 21st century: A balanced approach* (2nd ed.). Upper Saddle River, NJ: Merrill/Prentice Hall.

Vacca, R.T. (2002). Making a difference in adolescents' school lives: Visible and invisible aspects of content area reading. In A.E. Farstrup & S.J. Samuels (Eds.), *What research has to say about reading instruction* (pp. 184–204). Newark, DE: International Reading Association.

Venezky, R.L. (1995). Literacy. In T.L. Harris & R.E. Hodges (Eds.), *The literacy dictionary: The vocabulary of reading and writing* (p. 142). Newark, DE: International Reading Association.

Vogt, M.E. (1991). An observation guide for supervisors and administrators: Moving toward integrated reading/language arts instruction. *The Reading Teacher, 45,* 206–211.

Winograd, P., & Paris, S.G. (1988–1989). A cognitive and motivational agenda for reading instruction. *Educational Leadership, 46*(4), pp. 30–36.

Children's Literature Cited

Arrick, F. (1981). *Chernowitz.* Scarsdale, NY: Bradbury.

Avi. (2003). *Nothing but the truth.* New York: Orchard.

Coerr, E. (1977). *Sadako and the thousand paper cranes.* New York: Putnam.

Creech, S. (1994). *Walk two moons.* New York: HarperCollins.

Haddix, M.P. (1999). *Just Ella.* New York: Simon & Schuster.

Korman, G. (2003). The dive trilogy. New York: Scholastic.

Levine, G.C. (1997). *Ella enchanted.* New York: HarperCollins.

Lowry, L. (1989). *Number the stars.* Boston: Houghton Mifflin.

Lowry, L. (1993). *The giver.* Boston: Houghton Mifflin.

Reeder, C. (1989). *Shades of gray.* New York: Macmillan.

Rowling, J.K. (1998). *Harry Potter and the sorcerer's stone.* New York: A.A. Levine.

Sachar, L. (1998). *Holes.* New York: Farrar Straus Giroux.

Speare, E.G. (1989). *The witch of Blackbird Pond.* Santa Barbara, CA: Cornerstone Books.

Yep, L. (1995). *Hiroshima: A novella.* New York: Scholastic

Yolen, J. (1990). *The devil's arithmetic.* New York: Puffin Books.

Index

Note: Page numbers followed by *f* or *t* indicate figures or tables, respectively.

Q–R

S